While the last few of years have seen an in
malpractice—Christian leaders who shepherc
churches have not always been quick to recogni
I am so thankful for this new volume, Challe
resource that not only helps Christian institu
provides practical steps to address it. May God use it to protect and purify his church.

Michael J. Kruger
President and Professor of New Testament
at Reformed Theological Seminary, Charlotte, NC
and author of *Bully Pulpit: Confronting the Problem*
of Spiritual Abuse in the Church

In recent years the conservative evangelical constituency in the UK has been rocked by the exposure of abuse by several high-profile pastors and leaders within it. Some have been found to have been predatory sexual or physical abusers, whereas others have exercised pastoral power in a domineering, coercive or bullying manner that has caused severe psychological harm to the members of their churches. Denominations, networks, organisations, and local churches have quite rightly wanted to take action to prevent such abuse and care appropriately for its victims. This book is a valuable addition to the growing literature on what has been controversially termed 'spiritual abuse.' It draws together an experienced team of pastors, theologians, women's workers, and safeguarding professionals to help churches and Christian organisations identify sinful abuse of pastoral power. They bring biblical clarity to the definition of pastoral abuse, legal expertise on safeguarding responsibilities, pastoral sensitivity to victims of mistreatment and practical wisdom for investigating complaints fairly. This book ought to be essential reading for the leaders of churches and organisations, and will challenge and encourage them to foster a healthy culture in which everyone can flourish.

Rev John Stevens
National Director FIEC
(The Fellowship of Independent Evangelical Churches)

The soul-wrenching scandals of recent days have made pastoral malpractice the subject of more intense and urgent public concern. I pray that this book will help us, by God's grace, to prevent the trauma of abuse by and of pastors from ever occurring in the culture of our churches but also to handle this sin in a healthier way, with the godly seriousness it deserves, when it does rear its ugly, gospel-denying head. I commend it as a resource for the constructive conversations on this topic which church members and leaders all need to have.

Revd Dr Lee Gatiss,
Director of Church Society and author of
Fight Valiantly: Contending for the Faith against False Teaching in the Church

At a time when the fog of war has descended over the topic of spiritual abuse in the church, this work clears the air. Blending biblical depth, theological orthodoxy, gospel conviction, and pastoral concern, the authors navigate a field often dismissed by conservative evangelicals for miring itself in therapeutic language. And this is no church-bashing exercise: the love for the bride of Christ is obvious from start to finish. More than a textbook, this is a preventative manual, one worth reading with your leadership community. It will help you find safe passage through what is a cultural minefield, and better equip your gospel community to adorn the sound doctrines it confesses.

Stephen McAlpine
National Communicator: Third Space

A welcome contribution to the literature on pastoral malpractice in churches. This book is full of practical advice on creating a church culture that is healthy, positive and safe. I'm especially pleased to see it coming from the independent church community, but there is valuable guidance here for churches more widely.

Marcus Honeysett,
Author of *Powerful Leaders?*
When Church Leadership Goes Wrong and How to Prevent It

EDITED BY GRAHAM NICHOLLS

CHALLENGING

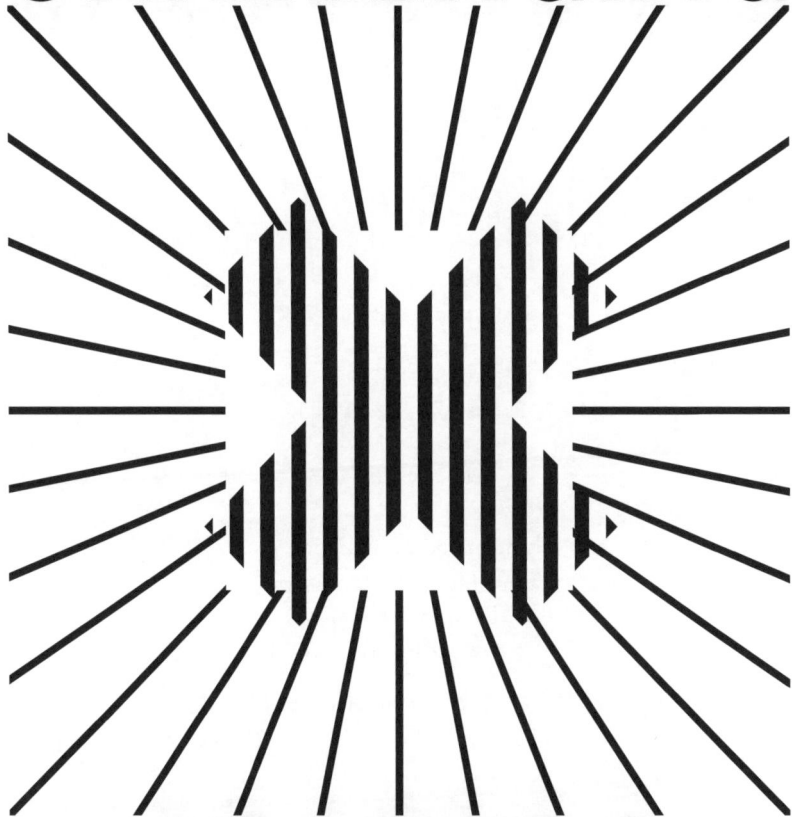

LEADERS

PREVENTING PASTORAL MALPRACTICE
AND INVESTIGATING ALLEGATIONS

CHRISTIAN
FOCUS

Copyright © Affinity 2023

ISBN 978–1–5271–1028-1
Ebook 978-1-5271-1030-4

Published in 2023
by
Christian Focus Publications Ltd,
Geanies House, Fearn, Ross–shire
IV20 1TW, Scotland
www.christianfocus.com

Cover design by Mark Steel

Printed and bound by
Bell and Bain, Glasgow

MIX
Paper | Supporting responsible forestry
FSC
www.fsc.org
FSC® C007785

CONTENTS

INTRODUCTION

Welcome to a resource for churches to help them in the complex area of what some have called 'spiritual abuse' or 'pastoral malpractice' – more simply put, the abuse of power by church leaders or abuse of those who are in power by church members.

Good spiritual leadership is vital to the health of the church. Leaders are to shepherd God's flock. In the vast majority of cases leaders, imperfect as they are, work hard with integrity, transparency and compassion. Likewise, their congregations love and respect them, even if they don't always agree with every action or decision.

Sometimes, however, that relationship breaks down. Leaders can misuse their position of power and be controlling, egotistical and proud, abusing the trust they have been given by the Lord. At other times, church members can become divisive and disruptive, 'mobbing' a leader, become over-critical, falsely accuse and even persecute those in leadership making it very hard for them to keep going.

In recent years, there have been a small number of high-profile church cases (and many others being dealt with privately), where charges against leaders have included an abuse of their power. Often the charges made are that leaders are acting in a heavy-handed way, or bullying. It is not easy for churches or outside bodies such as denominational networks to assess the validity of these claims because they are mostly about the subjective interpretation of behaviour, boundaries of leadership and discipline, and assessing patterns of behaviour rather than single instances.

We are now living in a cultural and regulative climate where there is far greater emphasis on recognising abusers and victims in child safeguarding, domestic abuse, and in the workplace. Relatively new terms have gained currency in domestic and leadership contexts such as 'coercive control' and 'power imbalance' and these are being read across to church leadership. Much of this is good. It shines a light on ungodly practice which may have been overlooked in the past.

Some campaigners would like to hijack the term spiritual abuse and use it as a quasi-legal term to denote criminal behaviour and to categorise aspects of normal, appropriate pastoral care including warning, admonition, and discipline as in fact abusive. For example, they might question whether people should be called to repent of sin and to change their thinking or behaviour, or whether the church should in fact, exercise discipline. In some instances, these biblical practices may be viewed as an abuse of individual freedom and identity.

Against this backdrop, there is a danger that church members may be confused and that leaders respond either with complacency or with fear.

They may dismiss all allegations of abusive leadership as stemming from the current cultural ideology that sees everyone as a victim and all power and privilege as bad. They would say 'there is nothing to see here' and take refuge in the fact that being a good and strong leader will always provoke opposition. But we must face the reality that in our fallen world, leaders do sin and need to be called to account; none are immune from falling in this way and leaders should be open to correction.

The Bible is not silent on the dangers of lording it over people as opposed to being good shepherds – it is a serious neglect of duty by church leaders. Abuse of power is not a new phenomenon, it is an ancient biblical category, as we shall see in the next chapter, and must be addressed.

On the other hand, leaders may respond with fear to the current climate of suspicion and become unwilling to lead in a biblical manner; they may end up tiptoeing around every pastoral controversy in case they are accused of heavy-handedness or worse. As confidence in biblical practice wanes, leaders may instead adopt policies based entirely on secular safeguarding models for good practice developed for businesses and charities which may have some merit, and indeed provide a defence against unwarranted accusations, but do not include the teachings of the Bible about sin, forgiveness and how the church should operate. Perversely this can often lead to a less loving and fruitful leadership as leading becomes an exercise in ticking boxes, while avoiding deep and open relationships.

We want to recognise there are cases where there has been a genuine issue of abuse of power. We also want to name abuse and slander with the language of sin, requiring repentance, and sometimes discipline rather than to lead with therapeutic or legal terms which can place it outside the normal decision-making of a church. This abuse of power can be individually carried out by a spiritual leader, or by a church member or group of members, and it can be enabled or ignored by systematic failures in church structures.

In our experience, clear moral failures are usually dealt with swiftly but issues of ungodly character and conduct are often allowed to continue. This is partly because of the difficulty of assessing the scale of the problem, but also because we do not value good leadership as we should. The very existence of this book affirms that abuse of power by leaders and of leaders does happen. It is wrong and we need to deal with it biblically, justly and compassionately.

It is for those struggling to navigate this hazardous landscape that we have produced this best-practice guide. It seeks to help churches work through these issues, to create a healthy Christian community in which concerns about pastoral malpractice can be raised and dealt with fairly, and in ways which are honouring to Christ, theologically faithful and legally compliant. It points to clear biblical teaching about how to recognise and develop good character in our leaders, and how to respond to serious failures.

We also want those who believe themselves to be victims of spiritual abuse to be confident and willing to come forward and to use this resource as a helpful reference to guide them.

We sincerely hope and pray that it will be a good resource for you and your church.

1

SPIRITUAL ABUSE AND SCRIPTURE

WHAT IS 'SPIRITUAL ABUSE'?

The term 'spiritual abuse' is a contested descriptor and therefore throughout this guide we will instead use the alternative terms 'pastoral malpractice' and 'abuse of power'. But whatever we call it, this is not a new extra-biblical category. This chapter explores the terminology and the practices it describes, looking also at the biblical censure of bad leadership and the responsibilities leaders have as under-shepherds. We will look at the evolution of the use of this term to provide some broader context for how we deal with it.

The language of 'spiritual abuse' is becoming more widespread. But while its profile is increasing, there is not universal agreement about its definition. We can trace the term 'spiritual abuse' back to the 1990s, when it was defined and developed by a small group of American authors. Their focus was on harmful Christian leadership practices that might be viewed very seriously by church elders' or members' meetings but that, for the most part, were not regarded as criminal.[1]

---

1. David Johnson and Jeff Van Vonderen, *The Subtle Power of Spiritual Abuse*, (Grand Rapids: Bethany House, 1991); Ronald Enroth, *Churches That Abuse*,

The practices identified with 'spiritual abuse' in these early sources included 'heavy shepherding' as a form of extreme micromanagement in pastoral care. Also listed were highly pressurised instructions to tithe or give more extensively, imposition of doctrinal norms without dialogue or debate, and development of a 'personality cult' around a pastor, minister or leader. The same authors also identified 'spiritual abuse' with intense expectations of loyalty to a leader or leadership team who allow little or no room for dissent.

Tragically, there is no doubt that such practices have occurred in some churches, and it is good that more recent studies in this area have built on the earlier American work from three decades ago to provide a fuller account of those practices, and of how to address them. While the term 'spiritual abuse' remains most prominent in this later work, other language has been suggested – both within that original American research and, of late, by the Evangelical Alliance, the FIEC, and others. We will explore that alternative terminology here, while recognising that 'spiritual abuse' continues to have the most common currency, particularly among those who suffer from the treatment it aims to describe.

So, let's start by exploring more fully what proponents of the concept of 'spiritual abuse' understand it to mean.

The academic psychologist Lisa Oakley and the CEO of leading Christian safeguarding charity ThirtyOne:Eight, Justin Humphreys, are among those who have expounded and promoted the concept of 'spiritual abuse'. Building on the formative American work cited above, and developing her own academic work with Kathryn Kinmond, Oakley teamed up with Humphreys in 2019 to

---

(Grand Rapids: Zondervan, 1992). See also Enroth's follow-up volume from 1994, *Recovering from Churches that Abuse*, (Grand Rapids: Zondervan, 1994. Downers Grove, Ill, 1993); Ken Blue, *Healing Spiritual Abuse: How to Break Free from Bad Church Experience*, (Downers Grove: IVP, 1993).

publish the influential book *Escaping the Maze of Spiritual Abuse*. There, she and Humphreys define 'spiritual abuse' as:

> ... a form of emotional and psychological abuse [that is] characterised by a systematic pattern of coercive and controlling behaviour in a religious context. Spiritual abuse can have a deeply damaging effect on those who experience it. This abuse may include: manipulation and exploitation, enforced accountability, censorship of decision-making, requirements for secrecy and silence, coercion to conform, control through the use of sacred texts or teaching, requirement of obedience to the abuser, the suggestion that the abuser has a 'divine' position, isolation as a means of punishment, and superiority and elitism.[2]

Although much in this definition could apply to abuses of power and authority beyond purely religious or 'spiritual' contexts, Oakley, Humphreys and others who echo them insist there is something so distinctive about the 'spiritual' context in which established criminal offences like Psychological Abuse and Coercive Control might occur, that it requires its own separate definition.

While they claim that 'spiritual abuse' need not itself rise to the level of criminality, the above formulation clearly draws on those criminal categories, and this has led others to critique their definition as too broad-brush – that is, as lacking sufficient nuance and precision. As things stand, Emotional and Psychological Abuse are defined in UK law as criminal abuses characterised by subjecting or exposing someone to behaviour causing or likely to cause trauma, including anxiety, chronic depression, or post-traumatic stress disorder. Within this definition, the term Emotional Abuse is usually applied to cases involving children, while Psychological Abuse is more typically applied to adults.

---

2.   Lisa Oakley and Justin Humphreys, *Escaping the Maze of Spiritual Abuse*, (London: SPCK, 2019), p.31.

The concept of 'Coercive and Controlling Behaviour' is a more specific form of Psychological Abuse that came onto the statute book in 2015, as part of the Serious Crime Act. It defines an ongoing pattern of bullying, threats, manipulation, humiliation, or intimidation used within the specific context of domestic relationships to harm, punish or frighten an intimate partner. However, as their inclusion of the latter term in their above definition of 'spiritual abuse' suggests, Oakley and Humphreys have been keen to see 'Coercive Control' extended beyond the parameters of the home to the church – that is, to relationships between pastoral leaders and congregational members and, presumably, between members. Indeed, they have more recently been active in seeking to add the language of spiritual abuse to Statutory Guidance on Coercive and Controlling Behaviour.[3]

Elsewhere in this guidebook, as part of the section on governance and policies, we provide a more detailed chart which defines different levels of abuse that might occur in religious or spiritual settings – one we trust will move the discussion forward constructively, and help Christian churches and networks deal with such abuses in appropriate ways according to their varied forms and contexts. Later in this current chapter, we provide a summary of the key headings used in that chart and suggest reasons why it might help to refine the helpful work already done in this area. For now, however, it is important to unpack a little more closely what makes abuse distinctively 'spiritual' for Oakley and Humphreys as opposed to abuse that might be identified more generally as emotional, psychological, or coercively controlling.

Oakley and Humphreys propose that for abuse to be deemed specifically 'spiritual' it must:

---

3. Section 76: https://www.gov.uk/government/collections/serious-crime-bill. Accessed 3/9/21.

- be 'justified' by appeal to the divine, or to one or more sacred texts defined as having divine authority;
- be enacted by people associated in their role or function as religious,
- take place in settings identified in one way or another as religious.

These criteria, of course, allow the term spiritual abuse to be applied to all religious traditions. It is only more recently, however, that the focus of academic research and writing on the subject has begun to look beyond the Christian faith.[4] Since Affinity is an evangelical Christian network, our focus here is on the latter – although it will become clear that the diffuse meaning of the word 'spiritual' within and beyond Christianity is one reason why some have looked elsewhere for more exact wording to describe the abuses in question.

Before we explore the implications of these points further, another terminological point is worth noting. Earlier books and texts on spiritual abuse tended to identify those who suffered it as 'victims'. More recent sources mostly define those who have managed to escape, move on or find healing from it as 'survivors'.[5] We see the case for each, and are happy to support either or both according to context – not least when that context includes the term preferred by those who have suffered the abuse in question.

This may seem all rather academic, but in reality it matters a lot. It matters because we need to be precise in what we mean when we use such terms as spiritual abuse but perhaps even more

---

4. https://www1.chester.ac.uk/trs/conference/spiritual-abuse/programme Accessed 24/10/21.

5. For a more detailed examination of the respective merits of 'victim' and 'survivor' terminology see https://www.ncbi.nlm.nih.gov/pmc/articles/PMC5426776/ Accessed 6/10/21; https://journals.sagepub.com/doi/full/10.1177/1077801218820202 Accessed 6/10/21.

importantly, it matters because we must be aware how others are using it, especially others who are not supporters of biblical Christianity and who are likely to define the term 'spiritual abuse' very broadly including normal church discipline and leadership and conflate the term with criminal and unacceptable behaviour.

RECENT CASES IN CHURCHES

As described above, it is recognised that much of what spiritual abuse seeks to describe is not unique to evangelical Christianity. Indeed, it resembles harm inflicted on many others who suffer bullying, manipulation and forced indoctrination at the hands of those who hold positions of power over them, whether the context of those actions is sacred or secular — let alone evangelical, liberal, radical, Anglo-Catholic or Roman Catholic.

Yet, it is clear from various high-profile investigations and reviews into the ministry of certain individuals, both in Britain and America, that this kind of abuse has indeed occurred in evangelical churches, and, sadly, may continue to threaten such churches unless more effort is made to spot, expose and address it. Controlling behaviour, bullying leadership and an expectation of unconditional loyalty have certainly characterised some of the ministries which have been in the spotlight under the definition of 'spiritual abuse'.[6]

---

6. For examples see:
   Mark Driscoll and Mars Hill Church: https://www.christianitytoday.com/ct/podcasts/rise-and-fall-of-mars-hill/ Accessed 10/02/2022.
   The Crowded House Independent Learning Review: https://thirtyoneeight.org/get-help/independent-reviews/crowded-house-review/ Accessed 10/02/2022.
   Independent Lessons Learnt Review concerning Jonathan Fletcher and Emmanuel Church Wimbledon: https://thirtyoneeight.org/get-help/independent-reviews/jonathan-fletcher-review/ Accessed 10/02/2022.
   Wymondham Abbey: https://www.churchtimes.co.uk/articles/2021/19-november/news/uk/bishop-of-norwich-orders-vicar-to-apologise-over-pastoral-breakdown-in-wymondham Accessed 10/02/2022.

The pain, hurt and trauma endured by victims and survivors of these harmful practices is disturbing and distressing. Such effects and symptoms of abuse in pastoral settings should be viewed with the utmost concern, and should be remedied as swiftly as possible, both through appropriate support for those harmed, and through preventative measures in safeguarding, governance and accountability that minimise the risk of such abuses occurring in future.

Later in this guidebook, we will provide practical advice as to how these measures can be put in place in your own local church.

Engaging with the Terminology

We want to be very clear that we take the core substance of what the term 'spiritual abuse' aims to describe very seriously indeed. The behaviours it refers to represent the real, felt experiences of more Christians than many might have imagined, and we lament that they have suffered as they have. We also recognise the momentum and purchase that the terminology of spiritual abuse has gained in recent years – particularly within the Christian Church.

Yet while we acknowledge the essential content of what spiritual abuse seeks to cover, we do believe that other, more precise language is available which we hope will advance our understanding in this area, thereby aiding victims and survivors. So, what are the alternatives?

'Pastoral abuse' was proposed as a variant on 'spiritual abuse' by Ronald Enroth, one of the American authors of the 1990s who first engaged in depth with the phenomena we are considering here. He made this suggestion given the church-based contexts in which the abuses concerned most typically occurred. Enroth's approach was 'both-and' rather than 'either-or': he used 'spiritual abuse' more frequently of the two, but it is significant that he was not wedded exclusively to it.

Others have developed and refined terminology based on Enroth's 'pastoral' vocabulary. As well as the Evangelical Alliance and the FIEC, the theologian David Hilborn, and the Christian author and leader Marcus Honeysett have found this language helpful. Indeed, we believe with these sources that the descriptors 'pastoral abuse', 'pastoral malpractice' and the more generic 'abuse of power' provide equally or more precise tools to describe this set of behaviours than the catch-all term 'spiritual abuse'. We also recognise that abuse of power can take place in churches against those in positions of leadership as well as being perpetrated by them, and that this dimension of abuse can be comparably harmful.

In a paper for a Chester University conference held in September 2021, David Hilborn proposed 'pastoral abuse' and (even more) 'pastoral malpractice' as better alternatives to 'spiritual abuse', arguing that they should even supersede it. He pointed out that while 'pastoral' is clearly a biblical word,[7] 'pastoral care' and 'pastoral teams' in schools, colleges or hospitals represent support offered by religious and non-religious people alike, so that 'pastoral abuse' in those and other contexts would not be an offence reserved to religious believers/spiritual practitioners alone.

By contrast, Hilborn argues in his Chester paper that the targeting of such believers and practitioners as distinctively liable for an extra category of abuse from which 'non-spiritual' people are exempt is a potential unintended consequence of the term 'spiritual abuse'. He adds that this could become problematic for religious liberties and inter-religious toleration in a secular civic society whose laws are otherwise designed to uphold religious freedom and prevent discrimination against people on the basis

---

7.   Cf. Ephesians. 4:11 and 1 Peter 5:2.

of their religion and belief – as, for example, in the Equality Act (2010).[8]

While noting these different approaches to terminology, and while supporting the ongoing refinements outlined above, this guidebook will use 'spiritual abuse' alongside the other terms we propose as appropriate, in recognition that for the moment, 'spiritual abuse' is the descriptor that victims and survivors most typically use. At the same time, we commend the fuller table of definitions supplied in chapter five, 'Developing Healthy Procedures' on our practice as an important contribution to ongoing work on this subject.

---

8. https://www.affinity.org.uk/news/617-reviving-erastianism-aspiritual-abusea-religious-liberty-and-the-paradoxes-of-post-christendom/
    In a yet-unpublished follow-up to this paper, Hilborn has further commented: 'It is important to register that the word "spiritual" is notoriously hard to pin down. It is used not only to describe the vastly different beliefs and practices of a whole range of religions in addition to Christianity; it is also increasingly appropriated today by people who claim no formal religious affiliation, but who strive for some sort of peace or meaning beyond themselves. That said, by definition, the concept of "spiritual abuse" still leaves significant numbers of hard agnostics, atheists, materialists and sceptics immune from ever perpetrating it. In that sense, for all the good intentions around its coinage, the term risks being used in a discriminatory way against people of faith – however "faith" is defined. Unlike much longer-recognised forms of abuse – emotional, psychological, physical and sexual – accusations of "spiritual abuse" can, *ipso facto*, only be levelled at a particular sub-section of the population: that is, those who align with the Spirit, spirits, spiritual disciplines or "spirituality". Normally, all citizens of a state are deemed to be equal under the law; in this case, some would be more equal than others. There is also a real risk that in an ever-more pluralist society, accusations of "spiritual abuse" might be wielded maliciously by fractious religious believers as a more benign-sounding cover for discrediting one another as heretics, infidels, bigots or radicals, or by non-believers hostile to religion as one more weapon in a mounting culture war between their secularist agenda and the missional ambitions of religionists'.

What does the Bible say?

Having discussed the debates about terminology and reality of the practice, we want to underline our conviction as authors that these ideas are not new to Scripture. Whatever terms we choose to describe it as, what we are talking about here all falls within biblical categories of ungodly behaviour – sinful behaviour from individuals, and in particular from leaders is all over the Bible, along with the contrasting behaviour of good leaders, supremely Jesus Christ. This means that the way we deal with allegations of pastoral malpractice should be subject to biblical scrutiny and that there will be principles that we must apply, with confidence (e.g. fairness of process, care for the vulnerable).

The Scriptures are clear that church leaders bear particular ethical and pastoral responsibilities for the Christians in their care. This makes emotional or psychological abuses perpetrated within the Church even more distinctive or aggravated. Indeed, biblically the standards to which church leaders are held are deemed to be 'above and beyond' those of other institutions and communities (Matt. 5:19-21; 1 Tim. 3:1-12; 5:7). Thus, the sense of hurt and betrayal can be intensified for a victim or survivor in such circumstances.

On one level, that intensification may be a difference of degree rather than kind (in relation to longer-standing definitions of emotional and psychological abuse). After all, the Bible recognises that we have emotions and a psyche ('soul'), that they can be assailed or oppressed, and that in certain cases at least, they are synonymous with that dimension of our being which is elsewhere called our spirit (1 Sam 1:15; Ps. 42:3-4; Matt 26:38). The point is not to deny that church-based abuse or abuse committed by church leaders might have a 'spiritual' dimension for their Christian victims. Nor is it to deny that this could compound what non-believers might experience purely as emotional and psychological abuse. Rather, it is to recognise that it would be unrealistic, and in fact unhelpful, to expect the state to legislate against any such spiritual dimension or aggravation of such abuse. Far better, in fact, to work with biblical discourse around abuse that does retain some traction in wider society today. To explore that, we need to start where Scripture starts our human story: in Eden …

- The Bible confirms that people have abused one another since the Fall in Genesis 3.
- The rebellion of Adam and Eve against God brought the corrosive dynamics of blame, accusation, dissembling, deceit and evasion into the world (Gen. 3:8-13). By Genesis 6 and the days of Noah, we learn that the 'wickedness of humanity was great' and 'every inclination of people's hearts was evil' (Gen. 6:5). In Jeremiah 5:30-31 a more specific picture is presented of what happens when such wickedness and evil are manifested in abusive leadership: 'The prophets prophesy falsely, and the priests rule by their own authority'. By the next chapter, this deception, power-mongering and egotism has curdled into counterfeit healing and pastoral care driven by the false bromide of 'Peace, peace,' when, in reality, 'there is no peace' (6:13-14). If anything, Ezekiel is even more scathing about abuse perpetrated by those called to be leaders: 'Ah, shepherds of Israel who have been feeding yourselves! Should not shepherds feed the sheep? You eat the fat, you clothe yourselves with the wool, you slaughter the fat ones, yet you do not feed the sheep.' He then sums up the damage done by such leaders in words that are as resonant today as when he pronounced them: 'The weak you have not strengthened, the sick you have not healed, the injured you have not bound up, the strayed you have not

brought back, the lost you have not sought, and with force and harshness you have ruled them' (Ezek. 34:1-4).

- These earlier prophetic warnings echo through Jesus' condemnation of toxic and hypocritical religious leadership in the Gospels and through similar warnings articulated in the Epistles. So, in Luke 11:39 Jesus condemns Pharisees who 'cleanse the outside of the cup' but inside are 'full of greed and wickedness'. A little later, the effects of undue religious legalism on ordinary adherents are condemned by Jesus as 'loading people with burdens hard to bear', while the legalists who propound them 'do not touch the burdens' with even one of their fingers. (Luke 11:46). Similarly, in Luke 20:46-47, the scribes 'like to walk around in long robes, and love greetings in the market-places and the best seats in the synagogues and places of honour at feasts,' yet simultaneously 'devour widows' houses' while intoning 'long prayers' as 'a pretence.'

- In Matthew 23, Jesus comparably condemns religious leaders who unduly 'burden' others without supporting them (v. 4); who 'shut the kingdom of heaven in people's faces' (v. 13), and who, again, hypocritically insist on petty legalistic observances while neglecting to show 'justice, mercy and faithfulness' (v. 23).

- In Luke 17:1-2 Jesus more specifically warns the disciples against those (in this context quite probably fellow-disciples or leaders) who cause 'little ones' to sin, where the 'little ones' are most likely either those young in faith, or young in years.

- In Mark 10:42-43, he contrasts existing Gentile rulers, who 'lord' it over those in their charge, with faithful Christian ministers who act as 'servants' to those in their care. Peter expounds on this same theme of servanthood when urging the elders among his correspondents to 'be shepherds [or pastors] of God's flock ... not greedy for money, but eager to serve; not lording it over those entrusted to you but being examples to the flock' (1 Pet. 5:1-4). The opposite of this would, by definition, be 'pastoral abuse' or 'pastoral malpractice'.

- Paul, likewise, lambasts religious 'empty talkers and deceivers' who 'upset whole families' and 'teach things they should not teach' (Titus 1:10-11). By contrast, authentic spiritual overseers are distinguished by the fact that they are neither 'arrogant' nor 'quick-tempered', by their being neither 'violent' not 'greedy for gain', and by their characteristic hospitality, goodness, prudence, uprightness, devoutness and self-control (Titus 1:7-9). This in turn aligns with Paul's depiction of healthy churches as communities of mutual service, respect, and care, called to follow the example of Jesus Himself (Phil. 2:1-11).

- Even when in certain contexts both Jesus and Paul also commend the exercise of church discipline (Matt. 18:15-17; 1 Cor. 5:5), they still do so with these fundamental qualities of humility, compassion, grace, and pastoral concern very much in mind.[9]

PASTORAL ABUSE IN RELATION TO CHURCH DISCIPLINE

It is important to stress that Scripture defines a whole set of additional abuses that have very rarely made it into the literature so far published on spiritual abuse. This is a vital point, because it

---

9. Cf. Johnson and Van Vonderen's advice that 'It is not abusive when a Christian (whether or not they are a leader) confronts another Christian because of sin, wrongdoing or even honest mistakes that must be corrected. The objective, of course, is not to shame or discredit, but to heal, save and restore'. *Spiritual Abuse*, p.24.

shows us that the Bible is clear that there are sinful behaviours that do warrant loving church discipline. It is not credible for evangelical churches to hold a position that church discipline should never be exercised on account of current trends that might tend to render it 'inherently abusive'.

What kind of things are we talking about here? Such sins include religious profiteering (1 Tim. 6:3-5), refusal to seek reconciliation after a dispute (Matt. 18:15-20; Luke 17:3-4), fornication and adultery (1 Cor. 5: 1-13; 6:9-20), doctrinal heresy or false teaching (Gal. 2:11; 2 Tim. 4:1-14; Titus 3:10; 2 John 9-11), blasphemy (1 Tim. 1:20), and idolatry (Rev. 2:16). These matters are often absent from the debate on spiritual abuse, but most evangelicals would agree that such offences are good grounds for loving church discipline – discipline, that is, which is motivated primarily by a desire to see the offender supported, rehabilitated, and restored to full fellowship.

ANALOGIES WITH OTHER MALPRACTICE

Those who have studied and written about spiritual abuse have largely highlighted that the phenomena described are evidenced in the work and ministry of religious leaders, and for our purposes here, of Christian leaders. As we have suggested, however, it is not clear that all the behaviours cited in the literature of 'spiritual abuse' are in fact specific to religious settings. In certain more serious instances, there might be a case for making an analogy with medical malpractice or misfeasance in public office and its related, more generic category: Abuse of Power. These are civil rather than criminal offences, often aggravated by the very fact that a role that entails a significant duty of care to others has been simultaneously exploited in terms of its designated authority and undermined by the distorted use of that authority.

Misconduct in public office, by contrast, is a criminal offence, and could perhaps entail a sub-category such as 'pastoral misconduct' or 'misconduct in a pastoral office' – although it might be argued that only ordained ministers in the Church of England would be subject to it, by dint of that church's established status in law and the related position of its clergy with respect to the state. In any case, the existing criminal categories of emotional and psychological abuse are available for any religious leader or adherent whose treatment, teaching, management, care or guidance of others is so egregious that it merits police investigation and, potentially, prosecution through the courts.

This underlines why it is problematic to use a vaguer and more generalised descriptor like 'spiritual abuse' to describe criminal behaviour like 'psychological and emotional abuse' and 'coercive control'. As we have emphasised, these have very particular legal thresholds and penalties associated with them, and unless abuse perpetrated in or around the church and/ or by Christian leaders reaches these criminal thresholds, it is better to avoid confusion with them in the language we deploy. Hence the more nuanced definitions we have advanced here as a refinement of the broader 'one size fits all' phraseology of 'spiritual abuse'.

Plainly, there is a range of other oppressive actions in pastoral settings that might not rise to the level of criminality, but that might still very well constitute a dereliction of duty and care demanding internal disciplinary action by a congregation, presbytery, council, diocese etc. Granted, there will sadly be some church leaders, elders, and others whose treatment of fellow believers and seekers is deemed to have broken the law. Far more likely, however, is conduct that will fall into this latter, sub-criminal bracket. This is not to say, though, that the harm such conduct causes will not still be deeply offensive to God.

Indeed, that is why this guidebook takes all levels and types of such abuse seriously, seeks to define them carefully, and suggests ways in which they can be effectively addressed – and better yet, prevented.

2

HEALTHY CHURCH
CULTURE

Prevention is better than cure. Creating and sustaining a spiritually-healthy culture is vital in the life of a church for many reasons, not least because it may help guard against the abuse of power by leaders or factions within the membership. Having a healthy church culture will not guarantee that abuse never occurs but it will contribute significantly to reducing the likelihood of abuse and the creation of a climate where concerns and allegations can be brought into the light without fear or favour.

In the next three chapters we will seek to answer two questions: what is church culture and what is a healthy church; before examining abusive church culture and describing how churches should care well for victims and alleged victims of unbiblical leadership. At the end of Chapter 4, a set of scenarios for individual reflection or group discussion are included and a set of diagnostic questions are provided for use in assessing the culture of a church.

WHAT IS CHURCH CULTURE?
Culture is a powerful factor in the life of any group or community, and any local church is no exception. What culture 'is' can be

difficult to pinpoint – yet we all have a take on the culture of any organisation or group we observe or are part of. Edgar Schein explains culture using the metaphor of a lily pond: the leaves and flowers are what's visible on the surface but whether or not they are healthy depends on a rich combination of factors which lie beneath and around them. In a church community there are obvious, visible artefacts and patterns (how people speak, dress, meet and so on) but so much more is going on: unseen and often unspoken assumptions and norms have a very powerful influence on the culture of that community and therefore what people experience when they are part of it.

Culture matters in the life of a church because it determines the answers to questions like:

- Who gets to belong around here?
- What is it okay to talk about?
- What norms are expected?
- How do things get decided?
- What is valued?
- What is derided?
- How is power held?
- How do those with power exercise it?

Biblical commands and exhortations are universal. But the application of them in a cultural context can legitimately vary in different settings.

Creating and sustaining a healthy culture is therefore important in the life of a church. Culture is not something we can 'do', rather, culture is what we get as the result of the way we do things. We can either be conscious and intentional about the way we do things in order to create a certain culture, or we can be habitual and unthinking and thus allow a culture to exist by default. Whichever way it comes about, the prevailing culture of your church or community has a huge impact on what it feels like to join, to participate and to exercise leadership. And although many aspects of the culture of a given church or community will be intangible – unexpressed 'rules' or norms of behaviour – it will be easily recognisable.

Paying conscious attention to culture is one of the ways that church leaders can help to prevent abuse from occurring. It is also one of the factors that must be addressed in any community where abuse has occurred or has been alleged and while every church or community will have unique aspects to its culture, reflecting its people, place and past, as Christ's people we are not left to imagine the essence of healthy culture.

Intergenerational and Cultural Differences

Different generations and different societies can vary enormously in their assumptions and expectations about relationships, leadership and authority. When a church family or staff team includes different backgrounds, a given conversation or action may be experienced in very different ways by different people, and result in a very different interpretation of motives. For example, a strong statement by a leader might be appreciated by some as providing clarity, while others may resent the perceived imposition of the leaders' views on their own freedoms.

These cultural differences about how to interpret behaviour also vary between different majority churches. A white majority church will be different from a black majority or Asian majority church. Some cultures where shame and honour are important can promote a healthy and thoroughly biblical culture of respect for the wisdom and status of older people but this might tip over into a demand for unquestioning allegiance to decisions by church leaders. Some smaller older churches might have established practices about how things should be done and family or friend networks, although not formally recognised as leaders might hold a strong influence over decision-making, especially where change is involved.

Similarly, differences between men and women need to be taken into account, embraced as valuable diversity rather than avoiding or silencing those differences. Complementarity affirms that men and women are equal yet different, so there will always be potential for situations and behaviours to be perceived and experienced very differently by men and women. While different churches will express their understanding of the 'equal but different' nature of men and women in different ways, a commitment to such complementarity may add its own complexity to relational dynamics, especially in contexts where leaders are all or mostly men. This makes it all the more important to pay attention to women's perspectives and ensure there are healthy ways for women's voices to be heard. The Bible teaches clearly that headship is to be marked by service and sacrifice, as Christ has done for His bride, and gives no scope for any use of authority which is oppressive or abusive.

It is vital to acknowledge all these differences. Unacknowledged, they can become a source of frustration, hurt, or resentment which can fester to become actual or alleged abuse. Leaders need to be willing to recognise these differences and explore what they might reveal about a church community; how they may shape perceptions of a church's culture, or how they may create the potential for (or support) the misuse of power.

No single generation or culture can claim to be perfectly biblical in its attitudes and practices, for we are all sinful people. So we cannot simply assume that the dominant church culture is infallible. Instead it would be wiser to encourage dialogue and reflection about generational and cultural differences, seeking to understand those perspectives rather than dismiss them. Healthy churches will welcome the different life experiences and world views of different generations and cultures, seeking to test them all in relation to God's Word and to integrate the valuable differences into life together: members of one body with different parts.

A church should not aim to conform to the surrounding contemporary culture, but neither can we safely assume that our internal church culture is perfect. Leaders need to recognise that when some members of our church community find that given approach to, say, leadership, decision-making or authority-jarring or concerning, it reveals something important either about the culture or the hearts of individuals, and usually both. Willingness to reflect humbly on those differences in the light of God's Word will help to avoid intergenerational conflict which can so easily turn into perceived or even actual abuse.

WHAT IS A HEALTHY CHURCH CULTURE?
'Healthy' Church

Often it is said that you will not be able to find a perfect church and if you do then don't join that church as you will ruin it! The truth is that we are all sinners saved by grace. We each, leaders and members, need to grow in godliness; to be transformed into the likeness of our Saviour. We are all works in progress; seeking to become more like our Saviour, the Lord Jesus Christ. Local churches need to strive to be communities where the gospel is lived out and to reflect the love of Christ more and more.

Where would you look in the New Testament to find an inspiring picture of a church, seeking to serve the Saviour? Such a church could be described as 'healthy' with a good, God-honouring church culture. John Stott suggests that in 1 Thessalonians we see 'the interaction which the apostle portrays between the church and the gospel. He shows how the gospel creates the church and the church spreads the gospel, and how the gospel shapes the church, as the church seeks to live a life that is worthy of the gospel.[1]

The church in Thessalonica had God the Father and the Lord Jesus Christ at the centre (1 Thess. 1:1b). The triune God is the source of the life of this church. The blessings that are sought, prayed for and enjoyed are grace and peace. (1 Thess. 1:1b). Paul identifies the marks of this gospel church – faith, hope and love (1 Thess. 1:3). John Calvin says these are 'a brief definition of true Christianity'.[2] With regard to the members of the church, each member is loved and chosen by God, individually and together. (1 Thess. 1:4). There will be suffering as they follow their Saviour (1 Thess. 1:6). Becoming like Christ is the aim of the church (1 Thess. 1:6). The gospel centredness of the church is a model to other churches. (1 Thess. 1:7). The gospel is the message that the church proclaims (1 Thess. 1:8-10).

As a church leader, you might think that the above are givens, that of course these are true of your church, they are the leaves and flowers visible to you and you hope to those who visit and join your local church. But what about the church culture below the surface? We need to look a little deeper.

A gospel-shaped, Christ-centred church in the twenty-first century, as in the first century, should always point to Christ and His saving work and be characterised as much as possible by praying for grace and peace. The church should be a company of people living out faith in difficulty; displaying hope when cast down and showing love for others. Every believer is to be valued, loved and chosen by God, whether they are weak or strong; young or old; the native or the stranger; rich or poor. No distinctions, no favouritism, no partiality; it is in our wonderful diversity we know unity and

---

1.   John Stott, *The Message of Thessalonians*, John RW Stott BST (Downers Grove: IVP, 1991), p20.

2.   ibid,, p 30.

together we can celebrate the love of Christ for the community of believers. A church like Christ will support the suffering, persecuted believer and preach, pass on, and proclaim salvation in Christ. The healthy church knows Christ alone transforms lives (turns from idols), enables service and perseverance (serves the living and true God), and looks forward to the return of Christ (wait for His Son from heaven). Encouragement is given to enable members to imitate Christ (1 Thess. 1:6). 'We need to look like what we are talking about ... we must embody it in our common life of faith, love, joy, peace, righteousness and hope.'[3]

'HEALTHY' CHURCH LEADERS

Immensely significant to the culture of a church, is the character and life of its leaders. Leaders are 'under shepherds', role models who give direction and set the tone of the culture of the church and impact members collectively and individually. As R. Murray M'Cheyne once said, 'It is not great talents God blesses so much as great likeness to Jesus.'[4]

While one can understand the ministry job adverts that specify qualifications and gifting that are requirements for ministry, these must not be sought at the expense of godly, Christlike character which is growing day by day in the leader's heart, mind, speech and actions. 1 Thessalonians 2 and 3 give insight into the Apostle Paul's pastoral heart. The Apostle Paul was not perfect, but he reflected Jesus, as should every leader in the church of the Lord Jesus Christ.

The Apostle Paul is known by the believers. Paul has already spoken of how the Thessalonians 'know him' (1 Thess. 1:5), and five times in chapter two he says they are his witnesses. (1 Thess. 2:1;

---

3.   ibid., p. 44.
4.   This quote is found in the article, 'Good News, Ordinary Pastor! You Don't Need a Winning Personality' found on 9Marks.org, accessed 27/7/21.

2:2; 2:5; 2:9; 2:10). Paul's life is one of service, sacrifice and suffering. (1 Thess. 2:1). He preached with integrity, knowing that God tests our hearts; he is a steward, entrusted with the gospel. (1 Thess. 2:4-5). Paul's demeanour and attitude are maternal, gentle and tender with the Thessalonians; as a mother cares for her children, he is sacrificial in his care. (1 Thess. 2:7-9). But there is a paternal aspect too, urging the Thessalonians to live a life worthy of the Lord; setting an example, teaching, training and encouraging the believers, even as he lives a life of holiness. (1 Thess. 2:10-12). Paul is a preacher and herald of the gospel, he commends it as God's very word. (1 Thess. 2:13). Paul loves the people he serves. (1 Thess. 2:20), he is committed to the Thessalonians (1 Thess. 3:10) and is prayerful. (1 Thess. 3:10-13).

This identikit picture of a leader is challenging and humbling. Church leaders are to display integrity and be 'known' by their congregations. They are accountable to others as well as the Lord; there should be transparency in life and ministry; before the Lord this will mean humility, coming from the heart and evidenced in speech and action. Leaders should speak and preach with integrity and truth, and not flattery. They are to encourage, comfort and exhort. Leaders must not speak harshly at home, to individuals, in church meetings or from the pulpit. They must not abuse the authority of teaching and preaching entrusted to them. Leaders mustn't use the pulpit as a platform for their own views, ideas and agendas. They are to be gentle, not overbearing, bullying or burdensome; leaders are to be sacrificial in their giving of time, care and concern and not be self-centred or autocratic at home, or in church life. Leaders must delight and rejoice in the work of God in the lives of those they serve. Leaders will be committed to the believers, they won't give up on them, and they will serve consistently. Leaders will pray faithfully for each member, praying for their spiritual walk and Christlikeness. A servant is not above his master and so there will be a willingness to suffer in ministry knowing that the Christian life is one of suffering now and glory later. Holiness is to characterise the leaders; there is not to be an abuse of money, sex or power. Often leaders have strong personalities, but leaders must put their confidence in the Word of God rather than in any charisma they may or may not have.

'Healthy' Church Members

We each make a contribution to the culture of the church, no matter how small we feel that may be. Many parts make up the whole. There is a collective responsibility. Members cannot simply blame others or the leadership for an unfriendly church or a church where individuals feel overlooked or even shunned.

In 1 Thessalonians 5:11, Paul instructs the believers to 'encourage one another and build each other up, just as in fact you are doing'. The church in Thessalonica is a community of mutual support. Paul has written to the believers so that as individuals they may live to please the Lord (1 Thess. 4:1-2); exercise self-control and be sanctified (1 Thess. 4:3-8); love each other (1 Thess. 4:9-12) and minister to each other within the family of faith (1 Thess. 5:14-15). When trials come, church members are to be comforted through grief and loss by the truth of the resurrection and the certainty of Christ's return (1 Thess. 4:14). Church members are to have relationships of trust, respect, love with their leaders (1 Thess. 5:12) and are to live at peace with one another (1Thess.5:13); worship together, rejoice, pray, giving thanks (1 Thess. 5:16-18), listen to the Word of God and not quench the Holy Spirit, test what they hear, hold onto the good and avoid all evil. (1 Thess. 5:19-22). Those in the church in Thessalonica are to pray for the apostles (1 Thess. 5:25).

The contribution church members make to the life, community and culture of a church is vital to its health and godly leadership will take up the responsibility to promote and encourage Christlike living both through teaching and by example.

Church members are told in Scripture to esteem their leaders as well as care and love for others in the fellowship. They are to pray for church leaders as they bear and seek to live up to the calling they have received from the Lord. Members are to thankfully receive the comfort, instruction and direction brought by leaders from the Word of God; holding onto the hope of heaven and the resurrection of all believers. Teaching is to promote thoughtful, discerning discussion and dialogue with church leaders in open discussion, enabling growth in Christlikeness. Members are to worship wholeheartedly, rejoice in their salvation and give thanks for God's goodness even in difficulty. Members have a responsibility to hold the leadership accountable and this can mean speaking out against pastoral malpractice or any abuse evident.

Paul ends this letter by praying:

'May God himself, the God of peace, sanctify you through and through. May your whole spirit, soul and body be kept blameless at the coming of our Lord Jesus Christ. The one who calls you is faithful, and he will do it' (1 Thess. 5:23-24).

Growing a Healthy Church Culture

We are all to ensure that our churches are as Christ-honouring and gospel-centred as possible as we place our confidence in the Lord Jesus who is utterly pure, blameless, caring and kind. He is the perfect chief shepherd, the faithful one.

Sadly, we realise churches are not always healthy Christ-honouring places. Churches and leaders cannot always be commended like the church in Thessalonica. Leaders can be abusive, (as well as abused), and those under their care can be harmed.

The diagnostic tool at the end of this chapter may help you to identify areas where your church culture needs to change and develop in line with God's Word. Humility, honest reflection, prayer, repentance, openness to criticism and correction, willingness to ask the hard questions, to be held accountable by others, and to develop links with other gospel churches are important in growing a healthy church culture.

In pastoral work, awareness of context is vital, so thinking of who holds the power in a situation and empathising with those who might feel intimidated or threatened is important. When you need to have hard or difficult pastoral conversations, prepare well not just in terms of content but also context, ask yourself the following:

- Where will you meet?
- Will the person you are speaking to feel awkward?
- How many will be present?
- Should a woman/man or younger/older person be present for accountability and to put the person at ease?
- Will the person you are speaking to have a friend or advocate with them?
- Is this context the best one to serve this person in a godly way?
- Whose benefit is this conversation really for?

Preaching may also be open to an abuse of power. It is a solemn and responsible task for which an account to the Lord will be required. Abuses of power may happen when a preacher strays from the parameters set within a passage into personal preference or opinion. Staying faithful to expounding God's work can be an important restraint to abuse of power in preaching. Asking for input from others, feedback and follow-up with individuals is helpful.

Church leaders need to recognise the value of developing their own emotional intelligence; the capacity to be aware of, control, and express one's emotions, and to handle interpersonal relationships judiciously and empathetically. This is a skill that leaders may need help with and feedback from others, male and female, in order to grow and develop. There also needs to be the willingness to apologise and to recognise that mistakes are made in interactions with others. This prevents isolated mistakes from becoming ingrained, wrong patterns of relating. Church leaders need to be aware of their own strengths and weaknesses. No leader is omnicompetent and healthy leaders will welcome and value the help and gracious challenge of others. Good church leaders will welcome constructive comment on their leadership style and look to work with others to grow in godly behaviour.

Scott McKnight and Laura Barringer in their book *A Church Called Tov: Forming a Goodness Culture that Resists Abuses of Power and Promotes Healing*, explore how churches can become toxic cultures and what makes a church 'tov' which is the Hebrew word regularly translated 'good'. Tov churches with a 'goodness culture' nurture seven elements: [5]

- Empathy and compassion
- Grace and graciousness
- Putting people first
- Truth telling
- Justice
- Service
- Christlikeness

A church with such a 'goodness' culture will enable members to safely raise possible pastoral malpractice or an alleged abuse of power. There will be a culture where any concerns are dealt with

---

5.   The following list comes from Brian J. Tabb in 'What Makes a "Good" Church? Reflections on *A Church Called Tov*', The Gospel Coalition, accessed 8/12/21.

wisely and fairly. Individuals must know who to speak to and what process is to be followed. Concerns about possible abuse are not to be hidden but should be acted upon or investigated no matter who is being challenged, and what the consequences might be.

A healthy church will develop a culture where questions can be raised about its leaders, without offence being taken or defensiveness displayed. Leaders will encourage and be open to questioning and to receiving comments, taking feedback and criticism well. Accountability processes both within and beyond the leadership team can be very valuable and should be encouraged. No leader can get everything right all of the time and there needs to be humility displayed in the light of this. Leaders embracing feedback will grow in awareness of the areas they need to change, and this can be an important move to handling the power they hold in the church. In a healthy church culture, leaders will be able to understand and apologise to individuals where unnecessary hurt has been caused. This may mean awkward and difficult conversations but working through this process with all involved should be the norm for a healthy church.

If there is conflict in church life, leaders may become defensive, shut down, panic, or want to ignore the difficulties and become passive. Alternatively, any questions raised can be recategorised as 'complaints' and a disciplinary procedure embarked on when what is needed is an open discussion to resolve a matter. Wisdom is needed from leaders and members alike. Leaders are not to be defensive in the face of apparent criticism, rather they should be willing to listen and learn from what is being identified and be open to another point of view. The intention will be to engage and not shut people down. A healthy church will ensure that questions, complaints and accusations are responded to appropriately as outlined in Chapter 5 on procedure. Clear policies will help church leaders to resist any temptation to overreact to 'questions' by categorising them as complaints.

What adjectives would you use to describe your church? Healthy, happy, united, respectful, caring, kind. Often churches want to be visionary, dynamic and happening. These are not mutually exclusive descriptions for a church that seeks to honour the Lord. Churches should prize the 'one anothering' and the building up that needs to take place within a family of believers.

Imagine what would make your church display a 'goodness' culture; to be healthy as described in 1 Thessalonians. Psalm 133 exclaims 'How good and pleasant when God's people live together in unity!' Psalm 133 makes it clear that it is possible and beautiful for God's people – leaders and members, men and women, young and old, vulnerable and strong, those from all cultures, of all personalities and social backgrounds to live in unity. This is a very powerful witness and testimony to God's character and being a community like this, has the promise of God's blessing.

It is important for churches to reflect on what changes are needed in their culture, make sure there is accountability in place, and where necessary implement necessary change. It is powerful when a church is praying and working together for God's glory for the good of all and when a church works together to see unbelieving people reached with the transforming grace of God. When these priorities are upheld by church leaders, often, internal difficulties can be worked through and mutual understanding results. There won't be a need to move into a formal procedure as described in Chapter 5. Every church, regardless of independence or denominational affiliations should have a publicised complaints process which enables concerns and complaints to be raised and dealt with. Chapter 5 outlines procedures to raise concerns. Proper procedures should be in place in every church and publicised to attenders and members. FIEC has an abuse and pastoral malpractice statement.[6]

At this point, it is worth mentioning that the practices and procedures outlined in the following pages should be helpful for individuals from all church backgrounds. Nevertheless, different denominations will have their own procedures for dealing with these challenging topics, and some will be better equipped than others due to their church structures, so be sure to also confer with trusted members of your own denominational background to discover what procedures may already be in place.

The freedom for individuals to follow the complaints process agreed by the independent church or the denomination is positive; it is entirely reasonable to raise concerns, necessary in a healthy church, and is not to be viewed as divisive. Such openness should be encouraged. Church leaders should respond with grace and humility and not with harshness, silence or withdrawal. Engagement in the complaints process should be viewed as positive and designed to be fair to all parties that are referenced.

If there is not a healthy church culture where concerns are addressed internally by the individual church or wider denomination or externally if legally required, then members and attenders have the right to 'whistleblow' to prevent a continuance of ungodly, sinful attitudes, speech and actions and to ensure an investigation. Whistleblowing is the action in which a person informs on a person or group or people (e.g. church leadership) who is engaging in an unlawful, immoral or ungodly activity to an outside body, who are able to take action to investigate and ensure that if there has been abuse or malpractice it ceases.

6.   To read this statement, visit https://fiec.org.uk/who-we-are/what-we-do/ministry-networks/abuse-and-pastoral-malpractice, accessed 13/12/21.

Marcus Honeysett in his book *Powerful Leaders?* sets out the disincentives for whistleblowing in a church context, namely; fear of isolation; a disposition to forgiveness; theological reasons. It can be hard to have the energy to speak out, when one has already experienced trauma, there will be emotional cost but before the Lord, there is a responsibility to bring abuse into the light; one's conscience will not allow you to keep silent; 'far from being immune, they (leaders) are more in need of godly rebuke and correction than anyone.'[7] Whistleblowing will take courage, conviction and can be at personal cost to the whistleblower but should be undertaken for the good of all involved and ultimately for God's glory.

The important thing with whistleblowing is that the process is known about and accessible in your church and that the principle of whistleblowing is recognised as something reasonable that may be necessary, and not as something divisive. Good whistleblowing process should be viewed as being positive, designed to be fair to all parties that are referenced, and an important component for maintaining good practice.

---

7. Marcus Honeysett, *Powerful Leaders?: When Church Leadership Goes Wrong and How to Prevent it*, (London: IVP Books, 2022), p 105.

3

ABUSIVE CHURCH
CULTURE

One of the most distressing things that can happen to a gospel church is that it becomes damaging to God's people. The idea of a gospel church developing an abusive culture sounds unthinkable but the hard reality is that it can and does happen. Instead of being a context of care, nurture and growth it becomes an environment of harm. The long-term distress that this causes and the damage to the witness of a church in the community will be deep and lasting. In this section we are going to look at what happens when a church goes bad and its culture becomes abusive. What is written here was distressing to write and may well be difficult reading. In his sermon, 'The Saint's Safety in Evil Times' Richard Sibbes wrote, 'The greatest sins of all are committed within the church, because they are committed against the greatest light.'[1] Sadly, this seems appropriate when an abusive church culture or subculture emerges.

We are indebted to a number of courageous survivors of abusive church cultures for their insight and help in explaining the trauma

---

1. Richard Sibbes, *The Works of Richard Sibbes*, Vol 1, (Edinburgh: Banner of Truth), p. 299.

that comes from the abuse of power in God's name. Here in this section, we describe some of the expressions of abuse in church life.

SPIRITUAL ABUSE

Safeguarding procedures in churches have raised awareness of some of the evil forms that abuse takes. Within the growing awareness of this you may also hear the term, 'spiritual abuse'. As described in chapter one, spiritual abuse is not currently recognised in UK law, and not a term the authors would want to endorse but is increasingly being used by Christians to describe their experience of the evil things that can happen in church. It's a phrase that suffering Christians often find helpful to describe the pain they experience when people who share their faith do evil things to them. The evil things done are often done in the name of God to coerce, threaten, frighten and above all control people, and this takes place in the context of a local church or Christian organisation. As both the abuser and the abused share the Christian faith, it suggests the nature of this type of abuse is unique with inevitably unique spiritual consequences.

At the same time, it is important to be wise as to how we use the term 'abuse' in connection with church. If it is used as a casual shorthand for anything that makes someone feel uncomfortable, or for every adverse experience in church, then it becomes a term that is so general and imprecise that it may become devoid of any real meaning. If the term 'abuse' is used indiscriminately like this, it may also end up undermining and minimising the nature of real abuse.

Similarly, the word, 'abuse' is so appalling that if it is used casually and applied to every time a person feels uncomfortable in church life, it may impact negatively on the way we speak out about sin or God's judgement. There are times when Scripture rightly speaks into our lives and exposes sin and these are uncomfortable times, but by God's grace these are necessary times. We must be careful of any attempt to equate 'abuse' with legitimate spiritual challenge so that we do not silence the church from being faithful to Scripture and speaking out about sin.

The trauma from abuse within a Christian context may do very deep and lasting damage to a Christian and so it is important that church leaders recognise the damage it may do. Sadly, there is often a lack of awareness of the effects of abuse that can take place in a Christian context. The wounds of abuse need understanding if there is to be recognition and care from godly leaders. The way abuse may affect a person's understanding of God, their ability to trust, worship, pray or read the Bible and form relationships and faith, need to be understood by those in pastoral leadership if churches are to become places of healing for those harmed in this way.

It is important to recognise God's response to those experiencing abuse. Darby Strickland in her book, *Is It Abuse?* makes a helpful connection between the Bible's use of the term, 'the oppressed' and abuse.[2] This takes us to the heart of God towards those who experience abuse as we see in passages such as, 'The LORD is a refuge for the oppressed, a stronghold in times of trouble' (Ps. 9:9). Likewise, 'You hear, O LORD, the desire of the afflicted; you encourage them, and you listen to their cry, defending the fatherless and the oppressed, in order that man, who is of the earth, may terrify no more' (Ps. 10:17-18). And again, 'The LORD works righteousness and justice for all the oppressed' (Ps. 103:6). The balance between what spiritual abuse is, what it may do to a Christian, and the heart of God towards those abused is crucial to a balanced and godly pastoral response to it.

In a healthy church you will find people that look to understand and care, with love and patience, for those caught up in the trauma of spiritual abuse. It is not uncommon for a church to find people damaged by abuse experienced in another Christian setting coming

---

2. Darby Strickland, *Is It Abuse?: A Biblical Guide to Identifying Abuse and Helping Victims* (Phillipsburg: P & R Publishing, 2020), pp 24-25.

for refuge. This is a great opportunity to show the heart of God towards the oppressed; to listen and acknowledge the evil that has been done in the name of God and to be generous in the way you respond to the unusual pastoral challenges that those hurt may bring to your church. Responding with the heart of God will make the church a redemptive community for those experiencing this unique distress.

EASY MISTAKES

A common, but serious, failure of a church leadership is to assume that their church could never develop into an abusive culture. It is a dangerous misconception that because a church has a good reputation, regular Bible ministry and an orthodox statement of belief, that it is safe from developing an abusive culture. But experience shows that this is naïve and an abusive church culture can develop despite these things being in place. Any church is potentially vulnerable to the descent into an abusive culture, and regular Bible ministry with a clear statement of faith is not an absolute insulator against it. Recognising that abuse can happen in any church is an important initial step in guarding against it.

A similar mistake is to believe that because a church leader is gifted or widely used in their ministry that they could never be abusive. It is easy to assume this kind of connection but as with all sin, gifting never insulates us from abuse. No Christian ever ceases to be tempted by sins because they hold office in a church. The most gifted church leader is as capable of the sin of spiritual abuse as any other Christian. There have been gifted church leaders whose lives have shown a serious disconnection between their public ministry and practice as a leader, and they have used their reputation as a smokescreen to hide their abuse. It is not uncommon for a 'gifted' church leader's abuse to be overlooked or explained away because of their apparent gifting. Or for there to be reluctance to challenge their abusive patterns out of a misplaced concern that it may damage the reputation of the gospel. Covering up or explaining away sin never prospers the gospel, it only ever leads to more sin.

At the same time, we must take care not to caricature an abusive church culture and think that it is restricted to church leaders and pastors in particular. Much of the current, popular literature being written on church abuse seems to focus on abusive church leaders and pastors in particular. Abusive church cultures may equally develop through a dominant family, a group or an individual in a church. If church abuse is only understood in terms of the damage a church leader may do, we will miss the damage that churches can do to their leaders too.

BULLYING OR ABUSE?

Stephen McAlpine has written an essay exploring a possible distinction between 'clerical bullying' and how it may be different to spiritual abuse.[3] 'Clerical bullying' is the result of, 'a hard-headed, emotionally unintelligent person who has found themselves in a church leadership position which affords them the opportunity to have their own way, and in which there are few, if any, safety brakes to temper their excesses.' He then describes spiritual abuse as being more specifically narcissistic[4] in its presentation. McAlpine's essay goes on to give an interesting description of a spiritual abuse in action. The abusive leader will be asking 'what can I use of these people and what they have to get what I want?' And what does

---

3. To read the entire essay, visit https://stephenmcalpine.com/clerical-bullying-and-spiritual-abuse-are-they-the-same-thing/, accessed 15/11/22.

4. Like the term 'abuse' we need caution about how we understand the term 'narcissist' lest we also popularise it by incorrect use and devalue its clinical meaning. It is helpful to recognise that it is a clinical term with clear descriptors relating to Personality Disorder. (Refer to 'Narcissist in the Diagnostic and Statistical Manual' (DSM-5) for example) .

he want? He wants control of these people. He does not want these people to have any sense that they might be in any area of life, superior to him, or more gifted. The basic building block of the spiritual abuser is to leverage what he has to control people. Anyone who he cannot control is seen as a threat.'

This distinction is worth considering. Both clerical bullying and spiritual abuse are evil but there is a difference between them. A pastor who misuses the privilege of the pulpit to criticise a member of the church publicly, or a church leader who loses their temper when hearing criticism about the church, or a church member who undermines the ministry of their pastor by lying about them to their friends are behaviours that will rightly be understood as abusive. But an abusive culture is more than moments of abusive behaviour, it is one which occurs when these kinds of behaviours become commonplace and sustained in the regular way a church functions.

POWER AND MISUSE

What are some of the indicators of an abusive church culture? Abuse of power is an obvious temptation to those who God has placed in a position of power as its leaders, but how power is held in a church can often be a complex thing. For example, longstanding or founding members, retired church leaders, a large family group etc. will often, in reality, hold more power than a newly appointed pastor. Always equating power with office is simplistic and an understanding of the way power works in a church needs careful consideration. Wherever there is power there is also the temptation to misuse power. Because of the legitimate power that goes with their office, church leaders will always face more opportunities to be tempted to misuse power.

Scripture provides examples of leaders that misused the power God gave them to serve their own purposes. A clear example of this is King Saul. In a helpful sermon Colin Smith[5] gives an analysis of Saul's abuse of his position and in doing so highlights many of the classic tactics of an abusive leader. In 1 Samuel 22 we read that when Saul heard that David had the support of four hundred men he responded with:

- Intimidation – 'spear in hand ... with all his officials standing round him' (v. 6).
- Obligation – 'Listen, men of Benjamin! Will the son of Jesse give all of you fields and vineyards? Will he make all of you commanders of thousands and commanders of hundreds?' (v. 7).
- Accusation – 'Is this why you have all conspired against me' (v. 8).
- Manipulation – 'None of you is concerned about me' (v. 8).
- Misrepresentation – 'Why have you conspired against me?' (v.13).

A more contemporary examination of Saul's behaviour would identify the classic abuser's use of passive aggression verse 6, gaslighting verse 13 and DARVO (Deny Attack Reverse Victim and Offender) verse 8. Saul's behaviour in 1 Samuel 22 is about using his power as king to control the men of Benjamin into meeting his personal needs.

The clearest indicator of spiritual abuse in a church is seen in how power is being used and what happens when those expressions of power are challenged.

POWER FOR GOOD

It is vital that any consideration of how power is abused is considered against the perfect example of our Lord's use of power. Here is the perfect example of a proper use of power.

---

5. To listen to the sermon, visit https://unlockingthebible.org/broadcast/the-deliverer-and-the-destroyer-part-one/, accessed 15/11/22.

Following His ascension and the coming of the Spirit at Pentecost, the disciples, as apostles, would become the most powerful leaders in the early church. It is significant that when Jesus gathered them together in the Upper Room before His arrest in Gethsemane, the first thing He did was to talk and demonstrate how power was to be exercised among them. Writing about that occasion John identified the absolute nature of the power Jesus had, 'Jesus knew that the Father had put all things under his power, and that he had come from God and was returning to God' (John 13:3). Immediately following this statement of absolute power we go on to read, 'so he got up from the meal, took off his outer clothing, and wrapped a towel round his waist. After that, he poured water into a basin and began to wash his disciples' feet, drying them with the towel that was wrapped round him' (John 13:4-5). The connection between the absolute power that Jesus has and His act of washing the feet of the disciples is breathtaking. It shows us what power and authority is to look like in the context of Christian community as it works in humility to serve others.

Jesus applies this lesson with a challenge about how His disciples are to exercise power, 'You call me "Teacher" and "Lord", and rightly so, for that is what I am. Now that I, your Lord and Teacher, have washed your feet, you also should wash one another's feet. I have set you an example that you should do as I have done for you. I tell you the truth, no servant is greater than his master, nor is a messenger greater than the one who sent him' (John 13:13-16). Like their Lord, the disciples are to use power for the good and wellbeing of others and not for self service. Following this example of Jesus, we go on to hear His revolutionary statement, 'A new command I give you: Love one another. As I have loved you, so you must love one another. By this all men will know that you are my disciples, if you love one another' (John 13:34-35). All of this is addressed to men being prepared for imminent leadership in the early church.

This principle of servant leadership coming from a position of power is seen in many places in the New Testament. Prior to the Upper Room example Jesus warned and indicated that His people are called to a radically different way of exercising power, 'You know that those who are regarded as rulers of the Gentiles lord it over them, and their high officials exercise authority over them. Not so with you. Instead, whoever wants to become great among you must be your servant, and whoever wants to be first must be slave of all' (Mark 10:42-44).

Paul in Philippians 2:5-8 encourages Christians to reject selfish living, 'look not only to your own interests, but also to the interests of others' (Phil. 2:4) and instead follow the example of Christ's humility and obedience,

> In your relationships with one another, have the same mindset as Christ Jesus: who, being in very nature God, did not consider equality with God something to be used to his own advantage; rather, he made himself nothing by taking the very nature of a servant, being made in human likeness. And being found in appearance as a man, he humbled himself by becoming obedient to death – even death on a cross!

When Peter writes to elders he encourages them to, 'Be shepherds of God's flock that is under your care' and the warning of, 'not lording it over those entrusted to you' (1 Pet. 5:2). The encouragement indicates that the power that comes from a Christian leader is for the pastoral good of others and the warning shows this power is to be held lightly.

POWER TO CONTROL

Commonly, abuse of power in church is often understood as a basic desire to control what takes place in a church and the lives of its members, for the benefit of the abuser. This is often understood as an abuser's desire to control others to serve the demands of their own will. It becomes about creating conformity to the desires of the abuser through their abuse of power.

Often when conformity to an abuser's demands is achieved, it is then reinforced with rewards in the form of acceptance or recognition within the structure of the church. These rewards develop a sense of belonging that will draw an individual more deeply to the culture. This is then often further reinforced by the use of critical comments about other churches or Christians that do things differently and this is designed to deepen the sense of belonging by feeling part of something special or elite. The process of control by reward may also take the form of equating conformity to an abuser with being regarded as mature, godly or being faithful to God. This becomes an attempt to build confidence in the abusive church system by encouraging a person to tie their understanding of godliness to the particular way the church functions.

Sadly, this kind of church culture may be very appealing to vulnerable people who are looking for security, acceptance and affirmation in general life. Vulnerabilities linked to lack of stability and security in their life are easily played on by an abusive power structure that offers the apparent comfort of acceptance and identity.

How far power is being abused will usually be seen when questions are asked, or criticisms made about the way the church is operating. In a spiritually abusive church culture, there will be little room for challenging questions to be asked. Questioning is quickly interpreted as a threat to power or authority and threatens the sense of control within an abusive culture. The more publicly the question is asked, the greater the push to regain control over them will be. In a healthy church culture, consultation and discussion are always welcomed. In an abusive culture, questioning is interpreted as a threat to control and its sense of stability and must be resisted.

Whenever the control of an abusive leader or system appears threatened, there will be a move to regain that sense of control. Often the initial move towards this will be seen in isolating or discrediting the source of the threat, irrespective of how supportive a person may have been in the past. This is about controlling the threat. This isolation can be seen in people being sidelined, ignored or overlooked. Though they may appear to be part of the church, the reality of their experience will be very different. Effectively this is punishment and it is usually sustained until they drop their line of questioning or objection. When this happens, it is not uncommon for the sidelining to stop and for them to feel welcomed back into the place they had before. This is about using punishment and reward to control people.

The fear of being left out in the life of the church, moved sideways, criticised or thought of badly by a leadership can be acute in people who have suffered adverse childhood experiences. An abusive culture will often offer a deep sense of belonging and identity that will appear practically appealing to vulnerable people and this may be done under the pretext that the church is special, and what is found outside their church is less than satisfactory, chaotic or even spiritually dangerous. People may be told regularly about the wonderful privilege of belonging to this particular church. When vulnerable or needy people are coerced into embracing this idea, fear of losing approval and acceptance become a major tool to control them.

Vision to Control

However, abuse of power may not always present so obviously as a leader's raw demand to control others. Other expressions of abuse may manifest themselves more subtly and some of these may have the appearance of being biblical and orthodox. For example, misusing power to coerce obedience to a vision that may be grounded in

Scripture, or conformity to a tradition that appears consistent with Scripture. While a vision may be legitimate, the means used to engage and mobilise a church to serve the vision, may include the abuse of power. In these situations, an abuser or abusive leadership may give the appearance of submitting themselves to the vision but will also be working to create conformity in the church by abusing power in the lives of others. This is an important reminder that expressions of abuse may not always be obvious when hidden behind the appearance of orthodoxy or enthusiasm for a vision, it may be overlooked for what it really is.

For example, the way a vision is implemented may place excessive demands on people in terms of time or financial commitments or there may be unreasonable requests made that make the church, family, work, and life balance impossible. Family life, career and financial security may be coerced into being sacrificed for the vision of the church. The demand of the church to fulfil the vision begins to take over the whole life of a person and if coupled to the idea that the church is 'special' or uniquely blessed, it can appear impossible to not agree to the demands being made. People then feel trapped and smothered by the intrusive demands that a church is making, but they feel silenced as the vision in itself is good. To question the demands being placed on them is to question the vision, and so it becomes an impossible situation where the only solutions are either to submit to the demands of the situation or to leave. This is coercion and control by misappropriation of vision.

Trust to Control

A further common method of control in an abusive context is the misuse of trust that may be seen in how valued information is managed in a church. Possessing information within a church is regarded as power and may be used to reward and control others. A distinction can be created between those who may be trusted to be, 'in the know' and those who are not yet up to being trusted. Information becomes a currency that reflects the degree of a person's apparent trustworthiness in the life of the church. So, if the church culture believes you can be trusted and are not a threat to the power balance in a church by not asking questions, you may be rewarded by being trusted with information. The information itself can be trivial or incidental but because it is shared selectively, it becomes a method of control by reward of trust. It may be as simple as being among those who get regularly invited to a leader's house after a meeting or talked to regularly by a particular leader at the end of a service or invited to a special prayer meeting. Being apparently trusted like this becomes equated with being special or part of something elite in the one being manipulated. Clearly for this to work there needs to be those who are excluded from being inside the circle of trust. Fear of being outside or removed from 'the circle of trust' can also be used to control and keep people in their place. An abusive leader will use this evil dynamic to keep people under their control.

The need for acceptance and to be trusted can be a powerful driver in all of our lives but an abusive church culture will look to exploit this. C.S. Lewis wrote about this phenomenon, though making a different application, in his essay 'The Inner Ring'[6] which is worth reading. This desire for acceptance and the appeal to feel special and trusted can be manufactured into an effective tool to keep someone, 'in their place'.

STRUCTURAL CONTROL

It is not uncommon when a church has an abusive leader or leadership for it to be structured in a way that promotes and preserves an abusive culture. The question of whether a particular

6. To read more about Lewis's conception of the inner ring, visit https://www.lewissociety.org/innerring/, accessed 15/11/22.

type of church government structure may be more vulnerable to being exploited by an abuser, is an important one and deserves consideration.

Listening to the survivors of spiritual abuse that so helpfully talked with us, several asked, 'Where do you go to in an independent church when things have gone wrong with your leadership?' This is an important question to ask of any church. An embedded abusive culture is unlikely to be open to help from a third party; for example, from the leadership of another church or a safeguarding organisation such as, Christian Safeguarding Services.[7] Third-party help can be a constructive way of highlighting failures in a church's processes and there are examples of churches that have been blessed by reaching out for help in this way. However, a feature of an abusive culture is that abusers within it will feel their sense of control threatened by a process like this and will resist it. Because of this there will not be a whistleblower policy for the church and more significantly there will not be an accountability process in place for leaders. The argument may be made that they are only accountable to God.

Because of resistance to accountability, it is unlikely that an abusive leader or leadership will engage in consultation with the membership, unless this process is very carefully controlled by them. The position that may be taken is that the leadership and its power is absolute and that it is the responsibility of the church to submit to this. An example of this we heard was a young man who was approached by a church eldership with a view to becoming a deacon. In the interview that followed the prospective deacon was asked if he had any questions for the elders. He did and after asking his questions, he was told that the offer of joining the diaconate was withdrawn as the elders felt his questioning of them meant he did

---

7.   To learn more about this organisation, visit https://thecss.co.uk/

not trust them. This is an example of a high degree of resistance to the mildest form of accountability.

As well as this, there may well be a reluctance for a church to be part of a wider network of other churches either locally or nationally such as Affinity, FIEC, EFCC, EA etc. The church may have adopted a practice that amounts to active isolation from other churches. In an abusive culture there can be suspicion of networking with other churches out of fear that a leadership may lose a degree of control within their church. At the same time there may be links made with other churches but on examination these links may well be with churches that operate similar structural controls within them and the arrangement becomes a reinforcing exercise. The links are often based on personal friendships where the feeling of trust is paramount. This develops mutual reinforcement between abusive leaders.

Structural concerns within an abusive church culture can be seen in how accessible its leaders are. There can be a contradiction between what is said publicly about the availability of leadership and what happens in practice. If a person is thought to be 'difficult' or overly questioning in the life of a church, it's not uncommon for them to find that the leadership is too busy to respond to them, or that any responses are brief and lack real engagement. This tactic is about wearing down the person asking 'awkward' questions and to effectively silence them by isolation.

Further to this, there may be a lack of transparency from an abusive leader or leadership to the general membership. Decisions may be made without the process being communicated; the need to explain the process is deemed unnecessary and threatening to their sense of authority or control. This can build a context within a church where having information becomes a source of power and control. We considered aspects of this earlier in the previous section, 'Trust to control.'

No church leadership structure will ever perfectly protect against spiritual abuse but being aware of how the way your own church is structured and what this looks like is a valuable exercise. The first step to becoming strong is recognising your own weaknesses. To this end, a practical (and curious) question that may be helpful to discuss is, 'if the devil were to try to develop an abusive culture in our church, would the current way we are structured be a help or a hindrance to him?'

Soft Control

Soft control is where an abuser uses power to subtly or indirectly control someone to bring them back to a place of control, without alienating or losing them in the process. Chillingly this is often about manipulating someone back under control, with a smile. Within soft control there is always the lurking presence of an implied but unspoken threat.

Responding to the threat of the loss of control over someone in the church, an abuser will often move to point out or reaffirm the apparent benefits that person is getting from being part of such a uniquely 'blessed' church. Talk about how God has been working in the church may be used to persuade a person that they must simply trust and stop questioning, if they wish to continue to be part of something that is regarded as elite or special. This tactic is about playing on a person's sense of belonging and identity with the blessing of God. Within this is the more sinister and implicit threat that to question the church or the leader, is to question God.

A similar approach is often used when questions are asked of a church leader where the response may be to warn the questioner by reminding someone 'Do not touch my anointed ones; do my prophets no harm' (1 Chron. 16:22). There may also be an attempt to point to a claim of unique gifting or to years of faithful and sacrificial service of a leader or attention may be drawn to a person's academic qualifications or their closeness to God as a leader. Usually this will be contrasted with the relative immaturity or vulnerability of the person they are dealing with. It becomes a move to highlight the weakness or immaturity of someone in contrast with the leader they are questioning. Past episodes of spiritual difficulty or failure that this person may have gone through may be referenced to prove this and it is not uncommon for issues shared in confidence to be now used more publicly to reduce the credibility of the questioner. This is about reducing credibility and raising uncertainty of anyone questioning the system in order to exercise control over them.

Another common tactic in soft control in a spiritually abusive system is to attempt to own or change the narrative of any questions being asked. Initially there may be the appearance of wanting to hear the concerns being raised, but the reality is these issues will not be engaged with. Instead, the concerns raised will be reframed in the conversation and replaced with the concerns of the leader. The intention here is to shift the focus away from the questions being asked and to draw a questioner into a different narrative. Often these concerns will be ones that no Christian would want to disagree with. For example, questions asked about how a Parent and Toddler work is being run could be replaced by a conversation to do with the need to reach more families with the gospel. The intention of this is to move the questioner away from the original issue that they raised and bring them to a point of agreement on a different issue.

Another way this may happen is seen in the way information is controlled and relayed to the church. For example, what someone writes in a letter of resignation may be 'summarised' and effectively rewritten when their resignation is communicated to the church. Invariably it will be done in a way that fits with how a leadership wants to be perceived by the church. The narrative within the resignation letter will be reframed to fit the narrative a leadership wants the church to hear. The issue here focuses on concern for the institution over concern for the individual to cover up ungodly practice in a leadership.

Frequently, people who experience soft control find the experience very confusing and exasperating. They know that they have had their say and at the same time they know their concerns have not been engaged with. They often find themselves being manipulated into agreeing to things they never felt were in doubt. At the same time there is a sense of threat and fear of rejection or exclusion. There will rarely be raised voices or direct accusations as the process is too subtle for this. However, this is about control through misdirection and confusion.

Some of these tactics of soft control may be familiar to you. You may have experienced them or you may recognise that sometimes you have responded to people in this way. You may be aware that this is the usual way your church behaves. Don't be complacent because of the word 'soft'. In reality those who experience this often find it is a gateway to deep feelings of helplessness and guilt that can haunt them for years. Despite the conformity that is coerced with soft control, the questions will linger or re-emerge in the mind of the one being controlled. The internal tension from knowing something is not right in the church but being controlled with soft threats can be deeply disturbing, particularly if within the abusive culture you see others experiencing hard control.

Hard Control

This is about more obviously destructive forms of control. It is about a direct approach often rooted in confrontation and accusation. If the tactics of soft control fail to produce the effect that an abuser desires, it will probably escalate to hard control. The tactics of hard control are used both to control an individual, and function as a warning to the rest of the church. Hard control will be used in an abusive church culture, but most likely it will be used rarely. If it is used too frequently it will become counterproductive by raising questions in others that may further threaten the sense of control within the system. Similarly, and chillingly, hard control does not need to be deployed regularly as the threat of it is sufficient to achieve the aim of control.

Hard control often looks to use fear, shame and humiliation to control an individual, and invariably it is exercised publicly to provide a statement to the church. Whereas with soft control the emphasis is often on the importance of the church and the value of being part of it, with hard control the focus is very much on the individual and their apparent failings. Similarly, with soft control there is usually a concern to keep a person on board and have them return to an abuser's position or point of view. In an unhealthy way, soft control becomes a restorative process to bring the person back under control. However, with hard control there is no interest in restoration as this is about attack with ultimate control being expressed by them leaving the church.

In the conversations we had with those who had experienced church abuse, some spoke of times where a leadership would actively ask people to leave the church. This may be done in a private conversation or publicly in a sermon. In our research we came across a situation when a pastor asked another (horrified) pastor for advice on how to get something like twenty church members to leave the church. The intention here is to control the challenge to power by removing people permanently!

The process of church discipline may also be abused to deal with people. This abuse of process is seen in the lack of any work towards restoration and the discipline becomes entirely punitive and not restorative. It is about putting people in their place, or even outside of the church. Because of this, it makes a mockery of the Bible's teaching on church discipline which is always for God's glory in the restoration of an individual, for example,

> Brothers and sisters, if someone is caught in a sin, you who live by the Spirit should restore that person gently. But watch yourselves, or you also may be tempted. Carry each other's burdens, and in this way you will fulfil the law of Christ (Gal. 6:1-2).

Hard control will be a direct attack on an individual who is understood to have stepped out of line. The attack will often be accusatory and take place in an environment that is controlled by the abuser to enhance their sense of control; for example, someone may be summoned to a church member's house or to a church office. It's not uncommon for the summons to be made formally and in writing rather than verbally, to add to the sense of control being exercised. As well as this, it is not uncommon for others to be invited to attend who may be supportive of the abusive church member or leaders. This is about building a context of intimidation and adding to the sense of control of the abuser.

Within this type of context, accusations are commonly made that go far beyond what is reasonable. A person may be told that they are 'doing the devil's work', or 'destroying the unity of the church'. These seem to be the two most common criticisms when things have reached this stage. It can even get worse with people accused of being under Satan's influence. Questions may be raised about whether the person they are attacking 'really is a Christian'. Aspects of their character may be attacked; they may be told that they are a 'troublemaker', or that they are being 'wilfully disobedient'. It may be asserted without any explanation or reasoning that they need to repent or apologise for their behaviour. A distorted profile of the person may be presented with apparent 'evidence' of their behaviour over a period of time and it is not uncommon at this point for issues shared in confidence to be brought up to build this profile. For example, attention may be drawn to any past difficulties in their family life that will be weaponised as apparent evidence of gross failure. In the process of our research, we heard of situations where this kind of intimidatory attack on a person's character would go on for a considerable length of time, with the appearance being to wear a person down. Invariably there is no dialogue within this 'process' as this is commonly seen as 'dealing with someone' and not about working for restoration.

As well as this, pressure will be brought from the wider church on the individual being targeted. They will find themselves actively excluded from aspects of church life by no longer being invited to events or cut out of regular sources of communication, such as being taken off the church's email or WhatsApp group. Criticism of their behaviour or details about their 'crimes' will soon become widely known and often with other 'loyal' church people joining in the criticism of them. It is not unknown for people in this situation to be referenced in preaching, whether by name or by being described in such a way that it is clear to most people in the church who is being referred to. The pressure from this process becomes relentless with the situation inevitably becoming intolerable for the person subjected to it and it will be sustained until their response becomes either to repent and get back in line or to leave the church.

Hard control like this is always abusive and is always evil. It grieves the Holy Spirit, brings dishonour to the cause of Christ and inevitably damages the reputation of a church in the community.

DOMESTIC ABUSE

Caring for the vulnerable is an admirable and necessary feature of a healthy church. Good church leadership will ensure that safeguarding policies for the vulnerable and children are in place and are followed. All disclosures of abuse must be dealt with seriously and appropriately. Churches have a legal duty to report domestic abuse to safeguarding services if a child is living in a home where such abuse occurs. Legally, the child is considered a victim of abuse. Always take outside, specialist advice and follow it through. It is an arrogant leadership that believes 'this kind of thing couldn't happen here.'

As part of safeguarding and good pastoral care, a healthy church will support those experiencing domestic abuse or domestic abuse survivors. Domestic abuse is a criminal offence.[8] Domestic abuse is complex, and this is not the context for a full treatment of it, but it is worthwhile for leaders to reflect that while domestic abuse is not necessarily spiritual abuse, there may be factors of spiritual abuse which are present. Do also consider whether domestic abuse may be a factor in a situation where there are concerns about, or accusations of other types of abuse. When domestic abuse occurs in a Christian home, the impact on an individual's faith; relationships and family life is deep and far reaching. Both men and women can suffer domestic abuse. It can be perpetrated by professing Christians and the Bible can be used to legitimise abuse within the home by perpetrators. Abusive behaviours are not permitted by Scripture, including restricting freedom to follow one's own convictions.

Church leaders can also create an environment for abuse in the homes of others through erroneous teaching and example. D. Eryl Davies details harrowing accounts of domestic abuse in the homes of those in church leadership in his book *Hidden Evil* where he makes a plea for domestic abuse to be a matter which is not overlooked by church leaders and includes guidelines for responding pastorally.[9] It is possible that through naivety or a lack of experience, church leaders may be neglectful or dismissive of a disclosure of domestic

---

8. To read more on this, visit https://www.legislation.gov.uk/ukpga/2021/17/contents accessed 13/5/22.

9. D. Eryl Davies, *Hidden Evil: A Biblical and Pastoral Response to Domestic Abuse* (Ross-Shire: Christian Focus Publications, 2019), p. 139.

abuse. Specialist advice and referral is available and should be sought.

In addition, to be a healthy church, reflection should be given on whether a church culture encourages or gives tacit approval to domestic abuse by the way in which women are treated or there is a bias against their disclosure of domestic abuse by a husband who is either a church leader, or is held in high regard for his gifting, outward moral character, Bible knowledge or teaching.

As part of seeking to be a healthy church, church leaders need to reflect on what should be put in place to positively support domestic abuse sufferers and survivors and ensure disclosures of domestic abuse from men or women are not quashed or disregarded. Church leaders in a healthy church should condemn domestic abuse when teaching on subjects like divorce, marriage, and family life. Davies makes a plea for there to be women pastoral workers in a church, trusted and accessible to the congregation, to whom a woman can make a disclosure without feeling intimidated and who is able to give appropriate support.[10] Helen Thorne includes guidelines for responding to disclosure in her book *Walking with Domestic Abuse Sufferers*[11] and provides a very helpful flow chart to follow when disclosures are made.[12]

The details of domestic abuse are complex and beyond the scope of this document, but please consider whether domestic abuse may be a factor in a situation where there are concerns about, or accusations of abuse. Sadly, there have been several publicised cases in reformed church circles that have treated survivors of domestic abuse wrongly. We can learn from these and ensure that survivors of abuse are cared for, supported and helped to heal, while always following appropriate safeguarding policies.

---

10. ibid, p. 166.

11. Helen Thorne, *Walking with Domestic Abuse Sufferers* (Downers Grove: IVP, 2018), pp. 35-36.

12. ibid., p 113.

4

TRAUMA AND THOSE
WHO SUFFER

This chapter defines trauma in the context of spiritual abuse and gives pastoral advice on how to care for those who suffer.

A legacy of trauma is often the result of the experience of abuse. As we have indicated, terms like 'abuse' and 'narcissist' may be used casually and sometimes inappropriately, to the point that they effectively become meaningless. The same may be the case with the word 'trauma'. Trauma has been described as, 'a psychic wound that hardens you psychologically that then interferes with your ability to grow and develop'. It is often associated with a literal or metaphorical 'brush with death' an experience of pain that is too much, too soon and too fast for the mind to process. The effect of past events may create a psychological wound that leads the sufferer to 'act out' that pain in the present, thereby damaging relationships in the present. It creates a legacy that is lived out in the way we process thoughts and memory, and its wounds are held and experienced in our body and in our mind.

Because God did not create us for trauma it becomes, in a perverse way, natural for us to experience its negative effects. We must be careful about pathologising the way our minds and emotions respond naturally to the effects of distress. Often we have the capacity to work through these negative effects naturally and particularly with the help of prayer, ministry and fellowship. However, there are times when the result of trauma becomes more prolonged and people may appear stuck in their distress, needing more specific and regular pastoral support. It is helpful to acknowledge that there is a distinction between what we might regard as our regular response to trauma and how we respond when trauma becomes a disorder. For example, in the case of Post Traumatic Stress Disorder it is generally regarded that about a month needs to elapse before the response can be considered a disordered response. However, a healthy church and leadership will look to provide support regardless of whether this might be regarded as a normal or disordered response and irrespective of the response, it calls for great compassion and intention to care.

Dr Diane Langberg, with fifty years of clinical and pastoral experience as a Christian psychologist has worked around the world with victims and often refers to trauma as, 'the greatest mission field of the twenty-first century'. That is, it is an opportunity to show the love and compassion of Christ to the broken. This helps us look positively at the evil of abuse by pointing us to the privilege of showing the heart of Christ towards those broken by abuse and for the church to be a place of safety, understanding, care and ongoing healing. The journey for a church to become a community of care may begin in the darkness of understanding abuse, but it will move to the light of knowing the heart of God for those abused in His name.

The trauma of spiritual abuse may well threaten the faith that, for the Christian, is their refuge against other forms of abuse. Instead of finding comfort in faith and fellowship, the trauma may create doubt and fear of things that were once most precious and make uncertain what were once fixed and certain convictions. It may distort a Christian's understanding of God and the church.

Those who experience the effects of spiritual abuse often live with the tension of looking for comfort in their faith but finding that faith to be also the context of their abuse. It may terribly distort a Christian's understanding of God and His body, the church. Christians who experience the effects of spiritual abuse often live with the tension between looking for comfort in their faith and their faith being the context for their abuse. They feel torn between wanting the church to bring care and healing to their wounds and living with the experience of it being something very different. So 'going to church' may feel similar to revisiting the scene of a crime.

With God's common grace there is specialised trauma help available and this needs to be recognised and signposted to by church leaders, but there is also much that a compassionate and trauma aware church leader and a church community can offer a survivor too. Often victims of this kind of abuse want to find a way back into the fellowship and support of a compassionate church community. They desire reconnection with the gospel life that may well have been torn away from them. An informed, healthy and compassionate church is uniquely placed to support a survivor on this journey, but finding the way back is not easy and the process may be easily derailed.

An indicator of the role that the whole church has in care and support is in the situation at Corinth when a man was put out of the church for gross sexual sin, 'of a kind that even pagans do not tolerate' (1 Cor. 5:1). Clearly this situation is different but what is helpful here is Paul's words later in 2 Corinthians when he returns to this matter with the words, 'The punishment inflicted on him by the majority is sufficient. Now instead, you ought to forgive and comfort him, so that he will not be overwhelmed by excessive sorrow. I urge you, therefore, to reaffirm your love for him' (2 Cor. 2:6-8). The church that inflicted the necessary wound of discipline now becomes the place of healing. Here the principle of how a whole church may be a place of healing for the wounds inflicted by a church, appears clear.

When caring for those hurt by abuse it is easy to feel ill-equipped but when daunted by the challenge, we need to remember God's heart is towards the oppressed, 'You hear, O LORD, the desire of the afflicted; you encourage them, and you listen to their cry, defending the fatherless and the oppressed, in order that man, who is of the earth, may terrify no more' (Ps. 10:17-18). This is the opportunity to show the love and mercy of Christ and remember that in God's providence, He has put these people in your church for you to care for them.

Here are some general things for you to consider:

Be Trauma Informed

Perhaps the starting point with this is for church leaders to become, 'trauma informed' or 'trauma aware'. Being trauma informed can mean different things to different people. For some it may mean completing a course of study or watching teaching videos or reading books, and these may be of great help and worth to a leader. However, it is easy to see being trauma informed as a tick box exercise. Being trauma informed is more about having a heart for those who have been oppressed and knowing how to recognise their distress and respond with respect and care. Crucially it is about knowing how to care and respond in such a way that does not re-traumatise them.

Central to a trauma informed response is the awareness that it is about bringing the care and reassurance of Christ, by being and offering the opposite of the pain that the trauma brought. So if the abuse they experienced looked to silence them, our care must give them back a voice. If abuse brought them pain, we must offer comfort in Christ. If their experience worked to shame them unjustly, our care must work to bring them into the freedom that there is in Christ.

1) Reassure and Accept

The main thing traumatised people need to feel about church is that they are safe. Feeling safe is a powerful move towards healing. But finding safety will take time (sometimes significant time) and only those affected will know when they feel really safe. We cannot overestimate the significance of a Christian, deeply wounded by the sin of a church or a leader, who begins to feel their way back into a church. A healthy church culture will look to welcome a survivor with compassion and patience but what a survivor needs at a time like this more than anything is time to feel safe. They need space to acclimatise to both you, as a leader, and to the church. Feeling welcomed is important, but so too is knowing that they can feel their way into the church at their own pace, with the permission and reassurance of the church. This means the church not pressing people with questions, asking for information or making demands of them, as often this will have been central to their experience of the abuse they suffered previously. It is important not to pry into what has gone on and to patiently respect the boundaries that someone may be putting up.

People who carry the wounds of abuse within a church setting may appear withdrawn, cautious and defensive, or may present as being evasive, angry or suspicious, particularly if they are in a new church setting. These are some of the ways that people will try to protect themselves from further pain. Often this approach works but it can also become a barrier to moving forwards and can leave them locked into the struggles they have. Acknowledgement, respect and gentle reassurance may go a long way to creating a context for moving forward from this. Working patiently to give time and space to a survivor can be demanding in its own way and particularly if they appear stuck on the edge of church life or uncooperative. It can be tempting to give up on people in this situation, or to overlook or even ignore them. However, ignoring a victim who is withdrawn is, in reality, pastoral neglect and will quite probably reinforce the trauma of rejection that a victim may well have experienced before.

A victim will often find the process of being in a church service challenging. As we have said previously it is like revisiting the scene of the crime. Courage is needed by the victim and this needs to be recognised by those who would look to offer love and support. There may be particular things that seem very straightforward to most Christians that can quickly trigger deeply painful memories in a survivor. For example, certain passages of Scripture or words may be difficult to experience for them as they will have been part of their abuse and weaponised against them. When survivors of oppression find themselves triggered, they will typically either become anxious or appear to drift off into their own thoughts seeming detached from what is going on around them. They may suddenly need to leave a conversation or service. It is important that we do not take these reactions personally or see them as being of great spiritual significance. Instead, it is the mind doing what it does when painful memories are triggered as it seeks to escape danger and look for safety. Because of these kinds of reactions, we must not underestimate how large a step forward it can be for a survivor to attend a church and we must look to be supportive.

It can be a temptation, when reaching out to victims, to attempt to be judge and jury about their experience; to try to make sense of what has happened and work out how to 'fix' it and all the more so when we find ourselves deeply moved by someone's suffering. This may satisfy your curiosity and possibly give a sense of emotional order to what you experience before you, but it will be of little help to the sufferer. What they often need initially is your acknowledgement of them and the reality of their distress. They may well have come from a situation where there has been denial, indifference or rejection of the pain they feel. Recognising someone's distress helps validate their experience and can be a great help to them feeling safe with you. We all need to be alert to the pressure we can feel to fix people. As people who care, we can want to step in to fix people, but we must seek what is best for the victim. Sadly, efforts to 'fix' traumatised people are often simplistic and may cause more harm than good. They can lack a servant-hearted approach and be more about the person offering support than the sufferer themselves.

So, initial steps are about reassurance through patient respect, and creating a sense of safety. From safety people can begin to explore trust.

2) Give Voice

Abuse works to take a person's voice away and to silence them by oppression; healing looks to restore it. Abuse takes power away; healing looks to restore power. Talking about, and listening to, what has happened is vital to healing the wounds of trauma. Often victims of abuse will have been told that no one will believe them if they talk, or that if they do talk people will just see how unreasonable they are. This is why we should never think of a victim in terms of just settling into church and moving on. Without giving voice to what has happened, there will never be any 'moving on'. Sadly, without finding a voice a survivor will probably remain stuck with the memory of what happened to them and the effects of this can run very deep into a person's mind and body. It could afflict them for the rest of their lives. Not allowing someone to give voice to the experience can be deeply destructive. An example of this is Kitty Hart-Moxon who, along with her mother, over a two-year period survived Auschwitz, other Nazi death camps, the notorious

Death March and finally Belsen before eventually arriving in England after the war. She and her mother were met by her uncle at Dover who quickly said to them, 'there is one thing I want to make quite clear. On no account are you to talk about any of the things that have happened to you. Not in my house. I don't want my girls upset. And I don't want to know.' Moxon went on to write about this, 'It may seem grotesque to say, after surviving the terrors of Auschwitz, that this was one of the unhappiest times of my life ... This was the nearest I came to total despair.'[1] It is a great kindness to help someone talk about their trauma and a great unkindness to close it down.

The kindest and most important thing we may do for someone when they are finding the courage to talk about the trauma they have experienced, is to listen. To listen well; fully and patiently. To listen without prying or trying to make sense of what they are saying. Listening well is another way of developing a survivor's sense of safety in a church. Knowing that someone is willing to listen and be present with them in their sufferings is the result of trust and trust is vital to someone feeling safe enough to talk about what happened. All our energy should go into supportive listening.

We should never be afraid to let someone talk about their trauma as difficult as it may be, both for them to talk and for us to listen. Often their experience of oppression from church will stir up fundamental questions about God and their faith. There may be anger expressed in this direction. It can be difficult to hear, and the temptation can be to try and answer these things for them. But giving expression to these painful, and even awkward, questions is often a step towards healing. Allowing people to give voice to fundamental questions can become an expression of trust. With oppression, the power to ask questions is often removed, so giving

---

1. Kitty Hart-Moxon, *Return to Auschwitz* (York, UK: House of Strauss, 2000), pp. 14,17.

permission to question the most fundamental aspects of our faith can be reassuring and liberating. We need not positively encourage doubts and questions, but we must allow it as it emerges. Of course, we will want to answer or speak into these questions and in God's timing the opportunity will come to explore these things together.

As a person puts into words what has happened to them and as they are listened to with compassion, their experience is being recognised and validated as being real to them. This is important, as often they will have been under pressure to deny or doubt their experience by their oppressors. It is not uncommon for someone who has been deeply hurt by the church to feel shocked at their own words as they begin to talk. At times like this, they need to be patiently listened to and reassured that talking is good. Conversely, a person may initially make a few light and even flippant comments about their experience and it is easy to get the impression that what happened to them doesn't really affect them. But this approach to talking is often a way of testing the ice, testing your reaction and seeing whether you can be trusted with more information. Never treat any talk of oppression lightly, it is evil and gently recognising how difficult it must have been for someone is helpful here. We must not push people to talk but be willing to listen as soon as they feel safe enough to talk, and we must always be willing to walk at their own pace and within their sense of feeling safe. Confidentiality is vital to this process and the slightest breach of this will probably shut down the process of talking.

Talking about what has happened is never easy and can be distressing both for the person talking and listening. It can often affect us in our bodies as well as in our thoughts and emotions and because of this it is wise to look for positive things that bring comfort. It will be different for everyone but things like taking exercise or listening to music may be helpful ways of calming the body when the mind has been engaged in painful memories.

The principle of giving voice to our distress is seen in Scripture and often a victim of abuse may find great help and comfort with certain passages as they give voice to the distress they have experienced. These words from Psalm 142:1-6 are good examples of this.

I cry aloud to the Lord; I lift up my voice to the Lord for mercy. I pour out before him my complaint; before him I tell my trouble. When my spirit grows faint within me, it is you who watch over my way. In the path where I walk people have hidden a snare for me. Look and see, there is no one at my right hand;no one is concerned for me. I have no refuge; no one cares for my life. I cry to you, Lord; I say, 'You are my refuge,my portion in the land of the living.' Listen to my cry, for I am in desperate need; rescue me from those who pursue me, for they are too strong for me.

Psalms like this are helpful in showing the legitimacy of giving voice to distress and the importance of being willing in this process to just be present and to listen.

3) Reframe

There comes a time when through the process of giving voice, a person will want to move towards making sense of what has happened and once again this must be at their own pace. This is about helping them to take control of the memories and their understanding of what has happened. Victims of oppressive church leadership will have been under pressure to think in a certain way and their voice silenced; this is the time to take back control over this and reframe all that has been said about and done to them.

Making sense of what has happened is not easy and takes a lot of time. The place of a compassionate church is to help repair a godly view of how a Christian understands themselves, the world around them and crucially of God Himself. This is something that a compassionate church community can uniquely contribute to and it can be important to a victim or survivor in moving from being a passive victim to finding comfort in Christ from their distress. The shock of rejection and the pain caused by professing Christians needs to be eclipsed by God's grace and truth, and the support of a compassionate church can be crucial here. This is about reframing what has happened in terms of their understanding of God, their relationship with Him and making sense of what has happened as a Christian. It is tempting to want to move someone into this stage to fix them but it cannot be rushed and must be at their own pace. If it is, it may shut down the earlier vital process of giving voice. It is vital that caring church leaders are wise enough to be patient and present.

Reframing is about moving on from focusing on what has happened to understanding the experiences in terms of our relationship with God. It is about exploring together the great points of reference that a Christian always has in any kind of distress. These would include the sovereignty of God, the providence of God, the faithfulness of God to His promises and the unfailing love of God. These are fixed and objective points that are always true irrespective of whether we are experiencing joy or distress and exploring them together within someone's trauma story may provide helpful truths, as they look to navigate what has happened. It is also about exposing the lies they may have been told about God. As with all of this, it is about exploring and maybe reconnecting with these truths about God at the pace of the survivor. This is why we talk about exploring and not teaching. Often church-based trauma will have had a strong emphasis on people having 'truths' forced on them. Changing the way that a person explores their faith to conversation and exploration can be helpful here.

This is a reminder that we should never have a completely negative view of adverse or traumatic experiences in life. The Belgic

Confession reminds us that all of the experiences in life come to us not, 'by chance but only by the arrangement of our gracious heavenly Father.' One of the more recently recognised features of traumatic events is Post Traumatic Growth. This is where people report positive change in their lives after going through highly stressful experiences. Maybe it causes them to think about life differently or to grow in appreciation for things they otherwise took for granted. Recognising this, we can go further as Christians in acknowledging that in every experience we go through, God is working for our good and His glory (Rom. 8:28). At the conclusion of the account in Genesis of Joseph's betrayal by his brothers we are told, 'but God intended it for good' (Gen. 50:20). The reframing of our memories of traumatic events with confidence in the good providence of God can be a major move forward in a Christian's growth and development. It is also why we should never view the experiences that come from surviving an abusive leader as wholly negative.

As well as these fixed truths there is the comfort of the moments in Scripture when we see God at work in His people's lives. Most comfort comes from considering the character and life of the Lord Jesus as He engages with those in need. Exploring the implications of Christ in Hebrews 4:14-16 as our great sympathising High Priest can be very fruitful. Even recognising the reality of sinful nature and Satan's work as the accuser of the Christian can bring understanding into the confusion of being abused by a professing Christian. This is not about having theological answers to a survivor's distress but moving to the place where a Christian may find healing. In all of this, it is important to remember that love, respect, and patience must be uppermost in our thinking as we look to support the move to wholeness and healing. We must not push these truths on people but walk at the pace of a victim or survivor towards them, gently encouraging them along the journey. We need to offer consistency and compassion.

One thing that may emerge in this process is a person's own sense of shame and guilt. There is never a perfect response to abuse and it is not uncommon for a sufferer to be carrying the burden of shame associated with anger and bitter feelings towards their abuser. Maybe, in what they have endured, there were times when they did not conduct themselves as a Christian should. For example, they may have been angry and lost their temper, and this can cause them to carry a legacy of shame. It can bring great relief to someone to talk about this and acknowledge their own failings but even greater relief will come through genuine repentance. It may seem inappropriate to be talking about repentance with a survivor of abuse but in reality, if it is done gently and in response to a sense of guilt it can bring great relief. The power of the cross and Christ's forgiveness can be wonderfully liberating to a survivor struggling with guilt over what they may have done or said. There can be great healing and restoration found through repentance where appropriate.

Within this process, a Christian will often struggle with the issue of forgiveness. In principle, this appears straightforward as we commonly pray, 'and forgive us our trespasses as we forgive those who trespass against us.' Forgiveness is a matter of the heart and conscience before God and because of this we can never push someone into it. Forgiveness is best talked about when someone begins to talk about it for themselves. For a Christian, forgiveness in the light of what Christ has done for them should be quite natural and it is very liberating. However, in reality forgiveness can often be complex. Can a person forgive someone who refuses to acknowledge the pain they have caused or who, worse, believes that the wrong they have done was right in God's eyes? Questions like this inevitably emerge and it is true that central to forgiving is the acknowledgement that wrong has been done. In asking these questions we must also ask if it is right for the closure and relief that may come from forgiveness to be held to ransom by a perpetrator's unwillingness to recognise the evil they have done. If we require an oppressor to first recognise their sin before we forgive, we run the risk of empowering them. Is it right for the victim or survivor to be denied the comfort that comes with forgiveness by an oppressor's refusal to acknowledge their sin? This is a helpful question to consider reflecting on.

Reframing is about moving forward and not being held prisoner to the evil that has been done to a person through the trauma of abuse. It is about gently encouraging conclusions about what has happened, that build a platform to move into the future. It is about exploring and receiving healing from God's Spirit. It is about recognising who they are in the eyes of their Heavenly Father and His faithfulness to them, about experiencing the freedom that comes from His acknowledgement of their sufferings and seeing a future with Him.

SEEING THIS BIBLICALLY

An example of this process in action is the Lord's dealings with Elijah after his showdown with the prophets of Baal on Mount Carmel. In 1 Kings 19, Elijah is clearly in great distress about Jezebel's threat to kill him. As he turns to God in prayer, we see that his perspective on what is happening is that he is the only faithful one left living in Israel. The stress that he is experiencing was probably exacerbated by his experience of confrontation with the Prophets of Baal and the lifting of the drought. This was, of course, a very positive experience but it included moments that must have been stressful. For example, seeing Israel apparently in the balance between faithfulness towards God or rampant idolatry (1 Kings 18:21) or seeing the self mutilation of four hundred of

Baal's prophets and their subsequent slaughter (1 Kings 18:28,40). Factor in the physical exertion of sprinting the fifteen or so miles to catch up with Ahab's chariot (1 Kings 18:46) and then running a further hundred miles from Jezreel to Bathsheba (1 Kings 19:3) where Elijah effectively collapses and asks God to kill him. It is reasonable for us to consider that though he was not abused, he was traumatised. It is clear, from what follows, that Elijah was carrying the legacy of the events at Carmel and Jezebel's threat in both his mind and body. He is overwhelmingly afraid (1 Kings 19:3) and suicidal (1 Kings 19:4) and James' observation that, 'Elijah was a human being, even as we are' (James 5:17) reminds us, among other things, that Christians can respond in similar ways when experiencing trauma.

The Lord's care of Elijah appears to follow a phased pattern similar to the one we have laid out in this section. Firstly, God cares for Elijah's body by providing him with food and encouraging him to sleep (1 Kings 19:5-8). He gives him time and cares for his body before he talks to him.

Secondly, Elijah is asked to present his complaint by twice asking him, 'What are you doing here, Elijah?' (1 Kings 19: 9, 13). Christ invites Elijah to give voice to his complaint and listens to him. Twice we hear Elijah tell God, 'I have been very zealous for the LORD God Almighty. The Israelites have rejected your covenant, broken down your altars, and put your prophets to death with the sword. I am the only one left, and now they are trying to kill me too' (1 Kings 19:10,14). As Elijah pours out his complaint Christ listens.

Thirdly, God reframes Elijah's understanding of his situation and what has been happening, 'Yet I reserve seven thousand in Israel – all whose knees have not bowed down to Baal and whose mouths have not kissed him' (1 Kings 19:18). He moves Elijah's thinking to what was true and to a place of hope.

Throughout this process, the Lord is reassuring and correcting Elisha with a view to effectively recommissioning him for future service, which we see in His instruction to anoint Hazael, Jehu, and Elisha (1 Kings 19:15-16).

Another very different context but similar example of this pattern is seen in Jonah 4 where we see God engaging Jonah, following the traumas of being thrown overboard in a storm, swallowed by a great fish, vomited onto dry land and then informing the capital city of the global superpower of his day (who happen to be Israel's enemies) that they are about to be destroyed by God, only for them to be spared.

Firstly, there is stabilisation: 'Then the LORD God provided a leafy plant and made it grow up over Jonah to give shade for his head to ease his discomfort' (Jonah 4:6).

Secondly, Jonah gives voice to his address identifying his perplexity and frustration with God, 'O LORD, isn't this what I said, LORD, when I was still at home? That is what I tried to forestall by fleeing to Tarshish. I knew that you are a gracious and compassionate God, slow to anger and abounding in love, a God who relents from sending calamity' (Jonah 4:2) and his suicidal ideation, 'He wanted to die, and said, "It would be better for me to die than to live"' (Jonah 4:8). 'I am so angry I wish I were dead' (Jonah 4:9).

Thirdly, we see God working with Jonah to reframe his thinking about what had happened, 'But the LORD said ... Should I not have concern for the great city of Nineveh?' (Jonah 4:10-11)

A healthy church culture will look to explore and develop this kind of phased approach to those who come their way carrying the trauma of pain inflicted by the church. The restoration of a survivor of church-based abuse is challenging, but very wonderful things can come from this. It is always vital to keep hope alive in the mind of a victim or survivor.

CARE OF ABUSIVE LEADERS

In Galatians 6:1, God tells us, 'Brothers, if someone is caught in a sin, you who are spiritual should restore him gently. But watch yourself, or you also may be tempted.' This shows how God would have the church respond to a Christian caught in sin. But what might this look like in the church's response to an abusive leader? This is not an invitation to go soft on sinful behaviour that would disqualify a leader, but in the light of the gospel we must always be willing to work for restoration.

Sadly, a leader who began well in ministry can lose connection with our Lord's example of foot washing by abusing the power Christ entrusted to them. In our 'cancel culture' world, it is easy to write off such a leader or use them as a lightning rod for unsanctified anger. A rarely asked but important question is what does the gospel have to say to this person? The gospel calls sinful people to repentance towards Christ to receive forgiveness and new life from Him, and sets the direction for what it means to live as a Christian. The gospel must frame our approach to abusive leaders; this begins with recognition of the evil done.

Many abusive leaders are closed to an offer of help and deny the effect of their behaviour, but those that are open to an approach must be responded to with the wisdom and care of Christ. The primary issue within this must be the recognition that what they have been doing is sinful. Any process that works for restoration and neglects or rejects this may easily be manipulated by an abuser to their own ends. Oppressive behaviour may be unintentional, but it is always sinful, and as with all sin it needs to be recognised for what it really is.

Recognised sinful behaviour should lead to repentance. Without being too prescriptive, we must consider what repentance may look like. We need to be aware that a manipulative abuser may use apparently correct words to smooth over what has happened to take the pressure off them. They may talk about change and promises may be offered, but it can be a smokescreen to what is actually going on in their heart. Authentic repentance will always recognise the evil that has been done to the people who have been hurt. This is why it is important to listen carefully to what is actually said, by way of repentance. There will have been sin against God and the church but if there is no recognition of the people hurt and what has been done, then it is inadequate repentance. Authentic repentance makes the connection between sins committed and the people harmed, with no excuses or reasons offered.

In Matthew 3:8, John the Baptist challenged the pseudo faith of the Pharisees with the words, 'produce fruit in keeping with repentance.' Genuine repentance is seen in how we live, what we do, and not only in what we say. Authentic repentance of oppressive behaviour will result in working for the good of those that have been harmed. The future and wellbeing of those oppressed will matter to them more than their own. What might this look like in practice? Again, we cannot be prescriptive, but we would expect the evidence of this to be proved and tested over an appropriate period. A few quick structural changes in the way a leader operates can become a smokescreen masking the reality of an unrepentant heart. Time must be allowed for them to 'produce fruit in keeping with repentance.'

Being more specific, we would commonly expect repentance to include a willingness to be held accountable in terms of any future ministry. Ultimately this would include a willingness to explore the question of whether they should continue in ministry. We would look for them to be open to substantial accountability regarding their ministry practice and this may be both formal, by way of new processes within the church, or informal, through greater openness and transparency within relationships in the church. There will likely be a new willingness to be questioned with an openness to receive, consider, and accept criticism.

By God's grace, there will be oppressors who recognise their sin and need for help and will be glad of it. They will need help to gain insight into the harm they have done and to move to repentance and reformation. In all of this they will need the help of those willing to descend the darkness in which an abusive leader will find themselves in their moments of self realisation. To be an under shepherd of Christ who is brought to see the damage they have done to Christ's flock is utterly dreadful, and to move from this place to a place of healing will need the fellowship of those prepared to walk faithfully with them. This is deeply challenging for those who would serve in this way and the strain on them may well mean they themselves will need support.

Within the work of gospel-formed care of an oppressive leader, there will be the need to explore the possibility that a leader may have become oppressive in response to things they have experienced in their own life or ministry that have remained hidden, isolated and unsanctified. These may be part of the baggage from life events that leaders bring to their ministry or a response to the adverse experiences they have gone through during their ministry. Left unprocessed, these may develop into attitudes of resentment, fear and insecurity that in turn may lead to oppressive behaviours as a way of dealing with them. Put simply, a leader deeply hurt by a powerful adverse church experience may become excessively defensive and manipulate those around them to protect themselves from a further similar negative experience. Or an emotionally immature leader may become self-serving and oppressive of others by regarding their ministry as a means to bring the recognition and sense of identity that they long for. There will be much more that will need exploring with an oppressive leader, but the issues identified here can be a fruitful area for discussion and are mentioned as they are often overlooked in responding to an oppressive leader. Sadly, situations like this do happen in churches and there are abusive church cultures. But it is our experience that there are many more churches where there is authentic fellowship, where leaders serve in humility with the willing and joyful support of the church. It's important to be reminded of this in the face of the dark things we have had to write about here. What we have written about here describes churches where evil things have become a normal and embedded way of working rather than occasions when a church or leader gets something wrong. It is important to recognise that this is not to create paranoia and doubt but to inform and encourage. The devil loves to hide in darkness and keep these kinds of practices hidden away. Instead of this, we believe the right thing is to bring them into the light and to encourage people caught up in these dark practices to walk towards the light, by looking for the help that will come when they take this step.

It is so important in all of this to remember that every local church is an expression and part of the body of Christ. To be part of a church, whether in leadership or not, is a great and wonderful privilege. The church exists for the honour and glory of Christ and never for the reputation of that particular church or its leaders or members. Christ's servants are called to follow their Saviour's foot washing example as they love one another as He loved them. The life of the people that make up a local church are to be, 'blameless and pure, "children of God without fault in a warped and crooked generation." Then you will shine among them like stars in the sky as you hold firmly to the word of life. And then I will be able to boast on the day of Christ that I did not run or labour in vain.' (Phil. 2:15-16), and it is only by looking to and listening to Christ with dependence on the Spirit of God that this is possible. By definition of what the church is and what we are as sinners, this means putting away sin and putting on Christ.

To make it personal for a moment as we close this section, if, in reading this, you recognise attitudes in your own heart, or behaviour that is ungodly, then we ask you to take your sins to Christ and make this first step towards the light of restoration. Because we are all aware of just how, 'deceitful above all things' (Jer. 17:9) our hearts can be, it is likely that you will need the support of other Christians as you journey towards repentance and reformation. We recognise that it is highly unlikely that anyone takes up leadership responsibility or becomes a church member to be abusive, though it is possible. We understand that sometimes it is our own story of difficulties in life that can lead us to be destructive to others, and we understand that it is so hard to recognise this, but it is important. Elsewhere in this handbook we look at some of the pressures that may work to corrupt us as a church leader or member and some positive responses to these, and we pray you will find these helpful. Please look for support as the great issue here is not the position you may have in church but the glory of God.

Similarly, if on reading this you recognise some of the evil things that were done to you in the name of God, we are glad you have had the courage to read this through to the end. You are brave and your experience was evil. Because of the intricacies of how these experiences may affect us, we are avoiding giving you simplistic solutions. Too much of this is offered by Christians who mean well but have little understanding of the realities of how trauma works. At the same time, we do have much to hold onto in Christ as we walk away from the darkness towards the light of recognising what has happened and the help that is available. There is some help available for you and elsewhere in this handbook we explore some of this. Above all we pray for you on your journey to wholeness.

'Do not let the oppressed retreat in disgrace; may the poor and needy praise your name. Rise up, O God, and defend your cause' (Ps. 74:21-22).

SCENARIOS

The following scenarios will help you to identify situations where care needs to be exercised and where there needs to be an alertness to a culture that could lead to pastoral malpractice. What these illustrate is that many times it is a fine judgement whether abuse or malpractice has happened or whether slightly clumsy application of appropriate leadership. In most cases, in trying to assess the cultural behaviour we will be looking for repeated patterns rather than single instances.

Following the Lead of the Elders

'Anytown Church' is a church with elders who are held in high esteem. They are 'shepherds of God's flock' entrusted with the leadership of the church, and are godly men qualified to lead according to 1 Timothy 3 and Titus 1. In Anytown Church, the elders bring proposals to the church meeting for discussion and endorsement by the members. To oppose a proposal is viewed as going against the elders.

At a church members' meeting, a new Assistant Pastor is proposed by the elders. A couple in their twenties, who are relatively new to the church, are unhappy with the proposal. Their interaction with the man being proposed has raised some questions in their minds. They voice their concerns in the open discussion prior to the vote. The members then vote by raising their hands. The couple vote publicly against the appointment, as does an elder's wife. Everyone turns to look at them, and visibly annoyed, the pastor says, 'Votes against: 3'.

Subsequently, interactions between the couple and the pastor are awkward; the pastor seems to avoid the couple and they feel unwelcome in the church. The pastor's wife never explained why she voted as she did. The couple hear rumours that people are talking about them, suggesting they are immature and disruptive. After a while, they leave the church.

Mentoring or Dictating?

'Somewhere Community Church' has a culture of 1:1 discipleship with older men and women mentoring younger men and women. A younger man seeks advice from the older man he meets with regularly. The older man is disparaging of a decision the younger man makes to date a Christian girl in another church fellowship and says she will not be a suitable wife for him. The advice is based on an assessment by the older man of the church attended by the young lady and the older man hasn't met the girl in question. The advice is given forcibly and unequivocally. The younger man goes ahead with the relationship; the 1:1 breaks down and the younger man feels ostracised and leaves the church. He subsequently stops attending any church for a number of months.

Elder – Pastor Dynamic

A younger pastor is appointed to 'Next Town Fellowship'. It's a smaller church and there are two other elders. The elders are older men who have both served faithfully at the church for over thirty years and see themselves as 'guardians' of the theological position of the church. One of the elders regards any change proposed by the pastor as theological drift and is unyielding in his views when any new proposal comes up. The younger pastor is in agreement with the core theological position of the church but believes some of his proposals are matters of tradition and practice, not theology. The other elder is hesitant and nervous and risk-averse and generally defers to his fellow elder. The pastor regresses to avoiding suggesting anything new and now dreads elders' meetings.

Women's Worker or Token Label?

'FarAway Evangelical Church' has employed a women's worker for the first time. Previously, the pastor's wife was responsible for women's work in the church, including outreach to women. From the start, the new arrangement proves problematic because the women's worker is struggling to fulfil the role she was appointed to, and the pastor's wife feels slighted, overlooked and unappreciated. The women's worker feels undermined in her ministry as the pastor agrees initially to her new ideas but then he often changes his mind, having talked things over with his wife. The women's worker feels she has little support from the elders, she hasn't got a mentor, and is left to work in isolation.

Discipling or Interfering?

Kate is a keen Christian woman in her late twenties with a burden to see younger women discipled. Enthusiastically she contacts four teenage girls from church families and asks them to join a book group for discussion and prayer. The youth worker, Pete, hears of this from one of the teenager's parents and is extremely put out. He writes Kate a strongly-worded e-mail and dismisses the idea, telling her that he has the discipleship of the teenagers in the church covered and her group is unnecessary and confusing. Kate is very hurt and upset. When she speaks to her friends, they suggest Pete is out of order, heavy handed and rude, that he has abused his position and is throwing his weight around. Kate doesn't know what to do next. None of the staff team seem open to criticism.

Adultery or Abuse?

A long-serving and much-loved pastor is found to be having an affair with a young lady in the church. He had counselled her when she was going through a rough time. The pastor confesses his wrongdoing and expresses repentance. He steps down from ministry and moves away. The congregation have great sympathy for the pastor because of his long years of service. In fact some of them still can't believe the affair took place and even if they do, they attribute the blame on the lady for entrapping him. Members who were loyal to the pastor think the elders dealt too harshly with him and some of them move to other churches. The remaining church members are pleasant but cold towards the lady and eventually she too moves away. The lady feels like a victim of abuse. She doesn't deny the affair was morally wrong but feels there was a power imbalance that is not being recognised.

For each scenario ask the following:

1. How is church culture contributing to the potential abuse of power?

2. Do you think some form of abuse has happened?

3. How would you want this dealt with?

4. What checks and balances should be in place to avoid something like this happening in the first place?

5. How could the church actively change their culture to be more healthy?

DIAGNOSTIC QUESTIONS

This diagnostic tool will help you assess where your church can grow in God-honouring practice. The following statements are to assess your church, your leadership and yourself in the light of 1 Thessalonians. Answer true or false.

A. God: Is the church God-centred?

1. Reverence for God is evident in worship.
2. The need for the work of the triune God; Father, Son and Holy Spirit is recognised in prayer and the life of the church.
3. The church members often speak about their relationship with Christ and all He has done for them.
4. Prayer expressing dependence on God is a characteristic of our times together.
5. Members are growing in Christlikeness. There is a willingness to talk about needs and areas where they are seeking to resist temptation and honour Christ.
6. There is a submission by leaders to the Word of God and humility is evident.

B. Love: Is the church other-centred?

1. Care and concern is expressed for all, especially the vulnerable.
2. Practical love is shown to the elderly, new mums, those in need.
3. A warm welcome is given to visitors and people seldom leave without being greeted.
4. There is an expression of concern for persecuted believers and the suffering church.
5. Favouritism isn't shown by the leadership.
6. Leaders are 'known,' approachable, and accessible and live transparent lives.
7. Leaders speak kindly to others and gossip, sarcasm and distasteful humour is able to be challenged by all.
8. Leaders sacrificially serve others and are seen to do so.

9. Members pray for their leaders, recognise their vulnerability and temptations and the heavy calling placed on them.

10. Care is shown for those in ministry; for their marriages and families.

C. The Bible: is the church Word-centred?

1. Good preaching and Bible teaching is at the heart of every ministry.

2. Biblical truth is expressed clearly with truth and love. Grace is extended.

3. Leaders speak with integrity and truth and are careful to base what they say on the Word of God.

4. People refer to what they are learning from God's Word rather than quoting the opinions of leaders.

5. There is a willingness to test, weigh and discuss what is being taught from God's Word.

6. Gentleness and patience are shown to those who are struggling in their walk with the Lord. Time, commitment, and practical care are invested by those in leadership.

7. People speak the truth in love when others face pastoral issues.

8. There is a readiness to apply God's Word of truth to every area of life and conduct.

9. God's Word being taught results in worship and thanksgiving.

10. Comfort, hope and consolation of the gospel are often shared.

11. The hope of heaven is held out to all, regardless of background, status, race, religion, past failures or present struggles.

D. Grace: Is the church grace-centred?
1. The need for the grace of God in our lives is expressed by church leaders.
2. People repent of sinful attitudes like anxiety, pride, complaining, fear of others, self-justification, bitterness, anger, and selfishness.
3. Leaders and members acknowledge wrong and ask for forgiveness where necessary from others – both in private and in public.
4. Areas of disagreement are worked through graciously by the leaders.
5. Any conflicts are resolved in a godly way.
6. It's okay to fail or get things wrong, mistakes are accepted.
7. Time off from 'ministry' is encouraged.
8. Care is given for the whole person.
9. Broken people are attracted to our fellowship.

E. Mission: Is the church mission-centred?
1. A welcome is given to all, unbelievers are not segregated.
2. Diversity is celebrated and the gospel is communicated to everyone.
3. The gospel is applied to the difficult areas of life.
4. The church is outward looking.
5. The church ministers to its local community.
6. It is clear to all that the church sends and supports those involved in missions around the world.
7. Time is given to the outsider, people are befriended and shown the love of Jesus practically.
8. The gospel is clearly understood and shared.

Reflection

1. Are there any attitudes or actions by leaders or church members you would like to see less evident?

2. Are there any attitudes or actions you would like to see displayed more?

5

DEVELOPING HEALTHY PROCEDURES

In this chapter, we will be looking at how a church puts in place procedures to ensure that complaints and concerns are heard and responded to in a timely, appropriate, and God-honouring fashion.

We recognise that some churches will be independent, and some will have denominational structures which provide help and also place certain obligations on a church when dealing with allegations. Church denominations and networks can also be of great help in writing policies and in any formal process of investigating a leader.

Whatever the ecclesiastical structures, there are a number of vital principles to bear in mind in developing policies and dealing with allegations of malpractice:

LISTENING WELL
James 1:19 instructs Christians to be quick to listen and slow to speak. This means that churches must be listening organisations who give a voice to people raising concerns regardless of whether the things they are saying are comfortable or uncomfortable to hear.

To this end it is essential that churches put policies and procedures in place to ensure that all complaints, concerns and feedback are accurately received, understood and responded to. Moreover, as we have been saying in the previous three chapters it is so important to develop a culture where church members are free to speak and express concerns, safe in the knowledge that they will be listened to and treated with care and respect.

JUSTICE

The God of the Bible is a God of justice. Nothing makes this clearer than the cross itself. The cross was the ultimate display of God's love (John 3:16) but it was also the ultimate display of God's justice as He punished the sins that had been left unpunished (Rom. 3:25-26). For God, love and justice must go together; it is impossible to be loving without being just as well. This works both ways – for the alleged abuser or defective team, and especially for the potential victim who may struggle to be heard.

God's heart of justice upholds the rights of the poor, the vulnerable and oppressed. As Deuteronomy 10:17-18 tells us: 'the Lord your God is God of gods and Lord of lords, the great God, mighty and awesome, who shows no partiality and accepts no bribes. He defends the cause of the fatherless and the widow, and loves the foreigner residing among you, giving them food and clothing.' Micah 6:8 asks: 'And what does the LORD require of you?' The answer: 'To act justly and to love mercy and to walk humbly with your God.' God is intensely concerned for substantive justice. He demands that the weak are protected and wrongs are punished. Justice must be done and will one day be done (Rom. 12:19).

The Lord is concerned with equal vigour for the demands of procedural justice. It is striking how many passages in both the Old and New Testament deal with procedural justice and the need for a fair hearing. In Deuteronomy 19:15-19, we read:

> One witness is not enough to convict anyone accused of any crime or offence they may have committed. A matter must be established by the testimony of two or three witnesses. If a malicious witness takes the stand to accuse someone of a crime, the two people involved in the dispute must stand in the presence of the LORD before the priests and the judges who are in office at the time. The judges must make a thorough investigation, and if the witness proves to be a liar, giving false testimony against a fellow Israelite, then do to the false witness as that witness intended to do to the other party. You must purge the evil from among you.

Justice demands not only punishing the guilty but also not punishing the innocent.

These concerns are repeated in the New Testament, where accusations against a fellow believer must be properly substantiated (Matt. 18:15-20) and accusations against an elder only entertained on the testimony of multiple witnesses (1 Tim. 5:19). With modern means of investigation, it is possible that corroborative evidence can be provided in multiple forms (video, electronic communication, DNA etc.) but the requirement for procedural justice must still be met.

Good Law and Good Process

In popular discourse, the priorities of substantive justice are often privileged above the priorities of procedural justice. Substantive law is about the rules and is used as a standard to measure behaviour. Procedural law is about the process of enacting and investigating allegations of breaking the substantive law. There is a tendency towards making a simplistic determination of guilt and ignoring process as something that gets in the way of resolving issues quickly. This can lead to a lowering of the burden of proof and an assumption of guilt. This has been used to justify trial by media and character assassination. All too often this has the lamentable consequences of wrongly punishing the innocent; and compromising legal process in the prosecution of the guilty and protection of the vulnerable.

It is essential that churches equally prioritise the demands of substantive and procedural justice. This is what our God of justice calls us to do. This is particularly important when the matter has been

The Six Pillars of Effective Safeguarding Practice

1 Policies	2 Procedures	3 Codes of Conduct	4 Systems	5 Culture	6 Integration
Intentional statements	Detailed instructions outlines what needs to happen.	How we expect all staff and volunteers to behave.	Record Keeping Filing	Intentionally formed	Safeguarding needs to be the DNA of the Organisation – NOT a bolt-on
Health & Safety	Accurate, clear and simple to follow.	Pastoral Care	Confidentiality	Pervasive across the organization	"the safety net"
ICT	Avoid jargon that would not be understood by the person who needs to follow them	Parents & children who attend groups	Reporting	Openness, Accountability & Transparency	Everything needs to be working effectively together in order to keep everyone safe
Grievances			Organizational Structure	Natural outworking of our gospel principles	
Complaints			Recording standards		
Compliments			Regular Review		
Disciplinary					
Safeguarding					
Whistleblowing					
Allegations					
Record Keeping					

CSS Christian Safeguarding Services — Training & Consultancy Services reported in the media or on social media. Decisions must be driven by the principles of justice, truth and transparency, not by public pressure. Resorting to a position that 'the end justifies the means' will inevitably lead to injustice and the undermining of the credibility of the process.

CATEGORISING COMPLAINTS AND ALLEGATIONS

It is tempting to think that all complaints and allegations should be treated in the same manner, but this cannot be correct. For example, a complaint that the music is too loud should be handled differently to a complaint that the pastor has sexually abused a member of the congregation. In determining how the complaint or allegation should be handled, the following factors should be taken into consideration:

1) The harm caused to the complainant
2) The harm and stigma caused to the accused if the complaint is upheld
3) Continuing risk to the complainant and others
4) The jurisdiction of other bodies to investigate and take action
5) The strength of evidence presented

In a church context, these factors mean that complaints / allegations fall into four main categories:

(i) Criminal offences

Crimes are offences established by Act of Parliament or common law which are deemed to be so damaging to society that they are prosecuted by the Crown (this is why the Crown Prosecution Service brings cases) and punishable by means which deprive a person of their liberty (i.e. prison). A moral stigma is attached to criminal offences which means that the standard of proof for crimes in English law is 'beyond reasonable doubt'. If someone is to be convicted of burglary, you need to be more than 51 per cent certain that they did it. Guilt must be established beyond reasonable doubt.

It is possible for pretty much any criminal offence to be committed within the context of church ministry, ranging from theft of stationary to murder. If there is any suggestion that a crime has been committed, the allegation should be reported to the police who should be allowed to conduct the investigation on their own timeframes. Any action necessary to preserve evidence should be taken. Nothing should be done to compromise the investigation or any future trial (including leaking information or making statements in the media – print or online). The church should do everything it can to assist the police and ensure a fair trial.

(ii) Safeguarding breaches

Safeguarding is concerned with helping everybody achieve their optimum outcomes, and churches will have systems in place to support people in this. Safeguarding breaches are recognised in United Kingdom law. Churches may encounter safeguarding breaches in two main ways:

1. A safeguarding concern: where the church identifies potential abuse and has a responsibility to report the risk of abuse to the statutory authorities.
2. An allegation: where there is a concern that an individual who holds a position (whether paid of voluntary) that requires them to provide care or support to a child, an adult with care or support needs,[1] or an adult at risk of abuse[2], uses that position to abuse the person in their care.

1. Adults with care and support needs are those who need help with day-to-day living tasks. This would include such things as cooking, cleaning the house, shopping, handling finances or personal care.
2. An adult at risk of abuse (sometimes referred to as an adult in need of protection) is an adult who has care and support needs (see footnote 1)

In line with the theme of this paper, we will focus on the second of these, however, it is important to remember that there is interplay between them, and that an allegation is likely to have involved harm (Point 1 above). The failure to appropriately report an identified safeguarding concern that meets the legal threshold is a safeguarding breach in its own right.

If there is an allegation or evidence of a person abusing a child or an adult at risk of abuse (as defined by the Care Act 2014) safeguarding procedures should be triggered in line with the provisions of the statutory guidance 'Working Together to Safeguard Children', the 'Care Act 2014' along with its guidance and Charity Commission guidance (or equivalent in devolved administrations).

The purpose of responding to safeguarding breaches is different from that of criminal justice. The criminal justice system seeks to punish crime with multiple objectives: retribution (requiring a criminal to pay for their wrong), deterrence (deterring other people from doing the same thing), reform (helping the offender to change), protection (protecting members of society from the offender), and vindication of the law (demonstrating that the law must be obeyed). The objective of responding to safeguarding duty is twofold: the protection of vulnerable people from harm and the promotion of their wellbeing. This means that the standard of proof is lower: on the balance of probabilities, i.e. more than 50 per cent; and that the remedies are more limited: only what is necessary to protect people.

Due to the importance of safeguarding and protecting vulnerable people, it is essential that criminal investigations and safeguarding investigations (by the local authority) take precedence over all other investigations and processes. In view of this, however,

and is at risk of abuse, and who, due to their support need, is unable to protect themselves against that abuse.

it is equally important that the narrow scope of safeguarding breaches is observed, i.e. as set out in the Education Act and Care Act. Even though we might use the term 'safeguarding' in a broad sense to describe protecting all people, safeguarding breaches are only those that fall within statutory definitions. We must be careful with our language. Although we might say that it would be a 'crime' for Manchester United to win the Premiership; we do not mean that an actual criminal offence will have been committed if they go on to be crowned Premier League champions.

(iii) Other statutory and regulatory breaches

There arc a whole host of other statutory and regulatory breaches that may be committed within a church setting ranging from failure to provide accurate financial accounts to health and safety violations. Churches are responsible to different government departments and regulatory bodies such as the Charity Commission, Health and Safety Executive, Companies House, HMRC, Home Office, the Information Commissioner's Office etc. Charity trustees and leaders should be aware of the relevant regulatory requirements, guidance, and procedures. If there has been a regulatory breach, the church should refer itself to the relevant body and seek advice.

(iv) Other complaints

We often refer to these complaints as 'sub-threshold' complaints since they do not meet the legal thresholds required for the three levels above. Abuse of power is often (but not always) in this area.

It is an incredibly broad category and will include trivial complaints such as 'I didn't like the illustration the preacher used'; to mid-level such as 'the leader always ignores me and does not listen to my opinion in the church meeting'; to very serious allegations: the pastor is having an affair, the assistant pastor is emotionally abusing a member of the church. The consensual affair with an adult is a very serious and disqualifying act for a leader (1 Tim. 3:2) but it is neither a crime nor a safeguarding breach (unless the other person is an adult at risk of abuse within the definition of the Care Act). It is important to say that this does not mean that the complaint is less serious or should be dealt with in a less rigorous manner. It simply means that a different set of procedures should be used. These will have different priorities, people involved and standards of proof. In this area of pastoral malpractice the seriousness and scale of any wrong behaviour might be difficult to determine – whether it happened, whether it was intentional and persistent and whether the complaint is reasonable.

Within this category of pastoral malpractice complaints, it is important to recognise that there are different sub-categories. These could include:

- Non-criminal 'abusive behaviours' that while harmful, do not meet legal threshold, often due to the fact that the victim is not classed as an adult in need of protection. This could include 'heavy shepherding' and the misuse of Scripture.

- Immoral behaviour, which while not illegal, would certainly be grounds for church discipline. An example might be an extramarital affair. (This might have the added complication that there is to some degree an imbalance of power, a duty of care neglected and a breach of trust.)

- Sinful or unsanctified behaviour, that is clearly not in line with Scripture, but which should be addressed pastorally. There may, of course, be situations where, due to impenitence, these ultimately result in church discipline, but initially, they would fall in the bounds of correction.

- Matters of conscience where a leader might be seeking to enforce their view on a church member on a matter where there is no clear scriptural teaching. This is an important category that must be handled well. By definition, leaders should not dictate on matters of conscience, however both wisdom, and clarity are required in determining matters that fall into this category.

- Genuine theological differences may also create complaints and require careful consideration, and wisdom and clarity are again required.

- Genuine misunderstandings are a further category, and in a healthy church, these should be resolved through honest conversation.

- Malicious or vexatious complaints are also possible, although it is vital that all complaints are taken seriously and examined. Too often, those raising concerns have been silenced through accusations of divisiveness, gossip and troublemaking. This is, however, a category that Scripture recognises (Deut. 19:15-21).

Charity Commission guidance expects churches to have a robust general complaints procedure which ensures rapid triaging of complaints so that the proper processes are applied.

Order of Handling Complaints

It is not uncommon for an accusation to be of an action which falls under multiple categories. For example, if a member of church staff is accused of sexually abusing a child it is an accusation of a crime, a safeguarding breach, a regulatory breach, a staff disciplinary breach, a general complaint, and a sin which will trigger church discipline.

It is important that order be observed. Where a criminal offence has been committed or a safeguarding breach that requires referral to the local authority has occurred, the nominated person within the church should be informed and the appropriate authorities contacted in accordance with the church's policies and procedures.

The Spectrum of Safeguarding

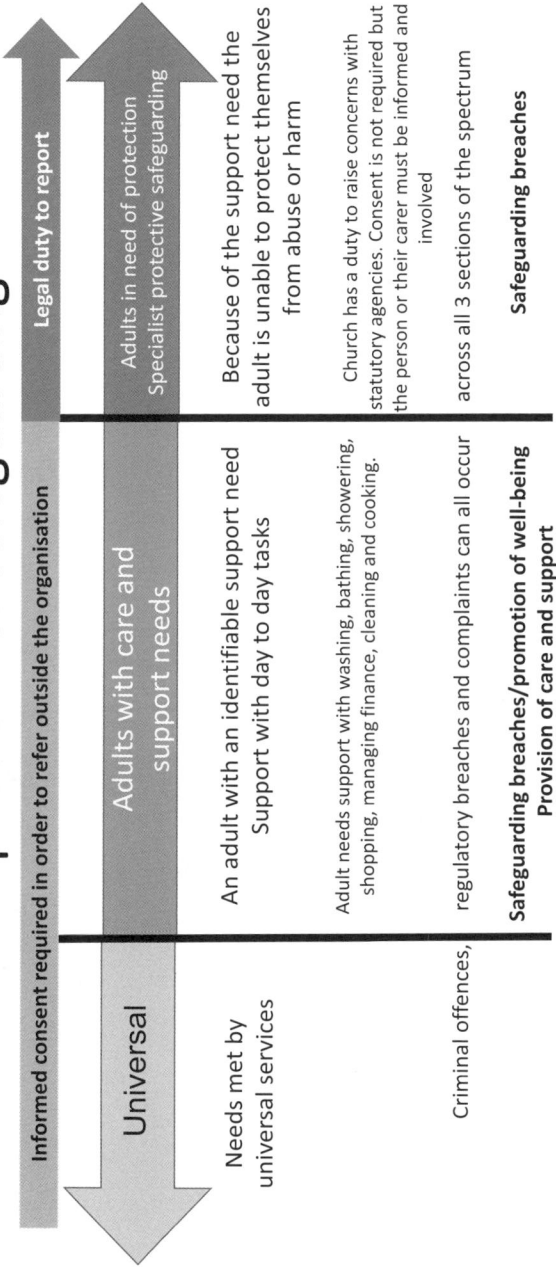

Informed consent required in order to refer outside the organisation

Legal duty to report

Universal	Adults with care and support needs	Adults in need of protection Specialist protective safeguarding
Needs met by universal services	An adult with an identifiable support need Support with day to day tasks	Because of the support need the adult is unable to protect themselves from abuse or harm
	Adult needs support with washing, bathing, showering, shopping, managing finance, cleaning and cooking.	Church has a duty to raise concerns with statutory agencies. Consent is not required but the person or their carer must be informed and involved
Criminal offences,	regulatory breaches and complaints can all occur	across all 3 sections of the spectrum
	Safeguarding breaches/promotion of well-being **Provision of care and support**	**Safeguarding breaches**

Table by Christian Safeguarding Services - used with permission

Immediate action to protect everyone involved or to preserve evidence should be taken without delay. The statutory services will advise, however, it may be necessary to impose some restrictions on the person accused until the matter has been investigated. This may include suspension of the member of staff or volunteer according to the procedures contained in the staff disciplinary policy. No further internal investigation should be made until the criminal and safeguarding investigation has been completed. Any statement made by the church must first be approved by the police / LADO / Adult Social Care Team and the person nominated by the church, to ensure that it does not compromise other investigations or legal processes.

When an incident occurs or an allegation is made, consideration should be given to whether the threshold for filing a Serious Incident Report with the Charity Commission has been reached, and whether the church's insurers need to be notified. Once criminal and safeguarding processes have been completed, any serious incident reporting can be finalised and a staff disciplinary hearing can be convened using evidence provided from other investigations, together with any new evidence that becomes available (the process for this will differ depending on whether the person is an employee or office holder).

Only after the staff disciplinary process has been completed should the church consider triggering church discipline. It is important to clearly distinguish the staff disciplinary procedure from the church disciplinary procedure. A member of staff may commit an act which constitutes gross misconduct leading to dismissal even though it does not lead to removal from church membership because the member of staff is repentant, e.g. drunkenness or sexual immorality. It is important that the staff disciplinary process runs its course before church discipline so that the different standards are not confused.

The Complexities of Pastoral Malpractice Complaints

Pastoral malpractice is a serious issue, and where the actions involve a crime or a regulatory breach, they must be referred to the appropriate agencies without delay. If there is any doubt about whether it has reached this point, advice should be sought. The majority of accusations of pastoral malpractice, however, are neither criminal offences, safeguarding breaches, nor other regulatory breaches. A pastor who counsels a member of the church in a heavy-handed and overly directive way may be a bad pastor and should probably be removed from church leadership, but they are unlikely to have committed a crime or a safeguarding breach (unless the person is an adult at risk of abuse within the definition of the Care Act 2014).

One of the complexities of pastoral malpractice is that accusations often implicate multiple members of the leadership team, meaning that the complainant lacks faith in an investigation carried out by the leaders of the church. It is wise to make provision in the general complaints policy to ensure the investigating officer and the person who adjudicates the complaint are independent, impartial and competent. It will often be possible to establish systems whereby such independence and impartiality is attainable within the church's internal structures. Inevitably, however, there will be some accusations which implicate all leaders within the church or where there is a belief that the church has a culture that makes it impossible for a complaint to be fairly heard. It makes sense to have provisions for external accountability in such cases. The tendency in recent times has been to use a safeguarding agency. This is usually inappropriate because the issue is not safeguarding-related and safeguarding agencies may not have the necessary expertise and experience to adjudicate on complex pastoral and theological questions. It may be better to have procedures in place to enable the complaint to be referred to another church or a denominational body in many situations. Each church should put in place external accountability procedures which are consistent with their church polity principles.

CATEGORISING CONCERNS

There are three types of concern that can arise in relation to pastoral malpractice. Those raising the concern may miscategorise their concern, and there can be overlap between them in practice. However, it is important that we correctly categorise the matter and deal with it according to the correct procedure. The three categories are:

- A complaint: An expression of dissatisfaction relating to policy or practice. It may be a concern that practice is inappropriate or unsafe, or it may be that policy and procedure are not being adhered to. Complaints can be about practice, culture or process and include unfair treatment. Complaints can expose systematic issues that need to be addressed.

- An allegation: A claim that an individual, who has access to children, or adults with care and support needs or at risk of abuse, has behaved inappropriately, has harmed someone, has placed someone at risk or harm, or that something about their behaviour would indicate that they pose a risk to others. Allegations focus on the person rather than the process and can involve an individual, or a group.

- Whistleblowing: Someone from within the organisation raises a concern that has been raised but not addressed effectively, or where they feel unable to raise the matter due to fear of the consequences.

The Outlines of a General Complaints Process

We strongly advise churches to create a robust process for dealing with allegations of abuse of power. In developing these procedures and practices, churches should be mindful of a number of issues:

Investigation Team

Any policy should set out who will investigate. This is probably already set out in your safeguarding policies for those kinds of complaints but for the allegations which are the main topic of this book it should also be clear. We would suggest that the default is that one or more leaders should investigate. This might vary depending on your church governance structures but we would advise that it is the church in the first place that should deal with any complaints or allegations. This is not to encourage a 'cover up', but because we believe that God has equipped the church with the competence and the obligation to carry out its own discipline.

Basis for Investigation

At the simplest level, a church needs to decide what is acceptable behaviour and what is unacceptable otherwise there is no basis for dealing with a complaint. In the content of pastoral abuse, there should be biblical standards set out which are both moral, and to do with character and behaviour. One of the ways to achieve this is to have a pastoral code of conduct which sets out general expectations for a leader based on biblical standards. A complementary document to consider might be a code of conduct for church members. The purpose of the investigation will not be to decide whether a leader has ever failed to meet the standards expected but whether the breach is significant in scale, duration and impact.

The policy should also set out in general terms what the possible response would be. For example, the investigation might result in the discipline of an elder by removal from office and/or a public statement acknowledging the issue and expressing repentance. Or it might be that no serious breach was found but there was a need for private repentance and reconciliation with any who had been affected.

Also the policy should explain what will happen if no wrongdoing is found.

In writing this we must be mindful that the goal of any investigation is not simply vindication of the survivor of abuse, or the accused. That might be part of it, but the main goal will be repentance and reconciliation brought about by a compassionate and just investigation.

Pastoral Care for Complainants

Making a complaint against a respected leader is often a courageous and scary act. There is a significant cost involved and the complainant may feel isolated and alone. Sometimes the process may necessitate that the people they would normally turn to for support are not available to care for them. For example, if the person makes an accusation which leads to a staff disciplinary hearing, a number of the church leaders may be required to sit on the disciplinary panel meaning that they are unable to discuss the matter with the complainant prior to the hearing. In such situations it is important that the church makes provision for the pastoral care and counselling of the complainant, either internally or externally. Where possible, the church should cover the cost of this as part of their commitment to loving and caring for the church member.

Procedures to Dismiss Vexatious Complaints

Sadly, it is not uncommon for churches to receive vexatious and unsubstantiated complaints. This can be used as a tool of abuse to harass and harm church members and leaders. While all complaints must be fairly heard and responded to, churches should put in place procedures which enable vexatious and unsubstantiated complaints to be dismissed at an early stage. Having a standard complaints form will ensure that evidence is collected and reviewed before a formal investigation begins.

Historical Abuse
It might be that a church member who has left a church a long time ago makes accusations against the leaders of a church, some or all of whom may no longer be in church. Such allegations must be taken seriously and investigated if appropriate with the spiritual well-being of those involved being of utmost importance. However, it might simply be that a fair investigation cannot be conducted due to a number of factors. These might include:

- the length of time since the alleged events making it unlikely there are people who can testify about what happened.
- the nature of the accusations are around culture, attitudes or perceptions which cannot be easily verified.
- the accuser is not in good standing or fellowship with a church and you cannot be sure of their motivation.
- the allegation if proved would not be of serious nature and would not have any impact on the current church leadership.

However, in a spirit of care and compassion any policy should place an expectation that all allegations are investigated as much as is reasonable and even if there cannot be an establishment of the facts there should be a generous and humble attempt to give the alleged victim a voice and weight carefully their complaint and seek to being reconciliation and healing.

Informal Resolution of a Complaint

In some cases, it may be possible to resolve a complaint by agreement with the complainant, without the need for a full investigation. This may, for example, be a concern about a procedure or practice. If, when the complainant raises the concern, it is agreed that this matter has been overlooked and needs to be addressed, then it is reasonable to simply agree the action that will be taken with the complainant, and then confirm when the agreed corrective action has been implemented. No investigation is required because the need to address the matter is not disputed and the complaint is not about an individual, so no right of reply is required. The handling of the complaint should still be recorded in accordance with the complaints procedure. If the complainant is not satisfied with the corrective action taken, the matter can be escalated to a formal complaint that involves a full investigation.

The Investigations

Conducting the investigation of a complaint can be a complex matter and the person responsible may feel out of their depth. Where possible a small support team should be created including leaders or other responsible individuals. It also might be useful to attend training courses.

However, we should not underestimate the power of the simple biblical instructions about verifying and weighing evidence and treating all with compassion and fairness.

In abuse of power situations, a lot of the investigation will involve listening to the people involved and weighing evidence. It will mean clarifying the substance of the complaint, by speaking with the alleged victim, with those who may have witnessed the abuse and comparing that with biblical standards and the code of conduct. In most cases you will be looking for more than simple yes or no answers, but to patterns of behaviour, expectations, and the degree and duration of any wrongdoing.

A report should be written up and agreed by the team, bearing in mind data protection laws might mean this report may fall into the public domain. The findings of the report should be shared with the church at the earliest opportunity but respecting the potential damage to individuals involved of putting too much information in the public domain, especially if the claim is not upheld.

Appeals

Churches should give careful thought to what appeals process is available for complaints. It is important to clearly articulate the grounds for appeal and an appeal should not be treated as a second hearing of the issue. We would recommend that appeals are only available on two grounds: (1) a procedural irregularity in the investigation or first hearing; (2) new evidence that has become available, for which there is good reason why it was not available at an earlier stage. To avoid vexatious appeals, we would recommend a standard appeals form which requires grounds for appeal to be stated at the outset.

Lessons Learned Review

It is important for church leadership teams and churches to learn lessons from events that have given rise to complaints. This should only happen once the investigation and relevant hearings and appeals have been completed. It is sensible to involve external parties in this, although it will be a rare event that would require the entire review to be conducted by an external organisation.

POLICIES

Along with a policy for dealing with allegations and complaints about the leadership discussed above, we recommend that churches have the following policies related to the handling of complaints and allegations:

- General Complaints Policy – for all church stakeholders (as discussed above)
- Safeguarding Policy – required by the Charity Commission.
- Whistleblowing Policy – enabling staff and volunteers to whistle blow on procedures or practice within the church which may be causing harm.
- Grievance Policy – complaints policy for staff which provides confidentiality and protection to staff.
- Staff Disciplinary Procedure – the procedure for hearing complaints against staff members.
- Pastoral Code of Conduct – document setting out the expectations and limits of pastoral ministry.
- Church Discipline Policy and Procedure – this will apply to all church members and usually be contained in the church constitution or rules.

Example Scenarios

Below are some examples to illustrate how an investigation might be conducted (or not!). We have included some examples above the safeguarding and/or criminal threshold for completeness.

Malpractice Examples

- The senior pastor is accused of bullying, harassment and intimidating behaviour towards junior staff and interns.
- A married member of staff engages in an extramarital affair with another staff member.
- The church officers / trustees make excessive demands of the church staff, resulting in some staff taking long- term sick leave due to mental health issues.

- A group of church members (in a church that has a formal membership) launch a social media campaign against a church leader, spreading misinformation and breaching confidentiality expectations but refuse to meet with the officers to discuss their concerns and resolve the matters in question.

- A member of the church staff is discovered accessing pornographic material (not illegal content) on a church computer during work hours.

- The church leadership are continually starting new projects and then pressuring members to give more, both financially and to volunteer in the ministries. They are applying Scripture in dubious ways to make members feel that they are not giving enough.

In each of the cases above, the concern relates to either the overarching duty of care to protect those who come into contact with the charity, from harm, or they represent moral / ethical issues that may require church discipline. Since the adults are not themselves Adults at Risk of Abuse or Adults with Care and Support Needs, (see definitions under 'iii Safeguarding breaches' above), this falls below the statutory threshold for reporting (although in some circumstances, a report to the Charity regulator may be required).

Although such issues fall below the statutory threshold for reporting, **they must be taken seriously and investigated impartially.**

In order to create a healthy environment where malpractice can be effectively identified and addressed the church needs to:

- ensure that clear processes, for ensuring that concerns about malpractice are heard and responded to fairly and transparently, are thoroughly embedded in the church life.
- ensure that the church culture enables the raising of concerns. This needs to go beyond merely communicating that it is 'OK to raise a concern' and should place an expectation on all members that they are required to raise concerns; both if they are concerned about the way they themselves are being treated, but also about the way that they see others being treated.
- ensure that the leaders provide a 'safe environment' that responds well when such concerns are raised.
- lay out clear standards of behaviour. This is traditionally done using codes of conduct; however, membership covenants and other means can also be used and may be more appropriate.

> The aim is to ensure that expected standards of conduct are outlined and understood both by those ministering on behalf of the church and also those being ministered to.

> If the expected standards of conduct are not understood by those ministered to, how will they know that a breach has occurred and that they should report it!

- ensure that relevant processes are triggered promptly.

The process for dealing with malpractice will be similar to that used for other formal complaints. The church leaders or trustees should ensure that specific allegations of malpractice are carefully investigated by a small team who are skilled, trusted and have sufficient independence from the alleged perpetrator to be able to make a fair assessment of the allegations / concerns. Agencies are able to provide training for churches that require this.

Informal Complaint: Resolution Achieved Without a Full Investigation

All expressions of dissatisfaction or concerns raised should be seen as an opportunity to learn, develop and improve and should be treated as complaints. If the complainant does not wish to raise a formal complaint, it should nonetheless be treated as an informal complaint.

- A new team member raises a concern with a ministry/ group leader about an aspect of the way the group is run. In discussion, it is agreed that this perspective has been overlooked and not considered in the past. The group leader agrees to consider the matter and arranges a further discussion the following week, recording the details of the conversation and confirming with the new member that this is an accurate and complete record of the discussion. When they meet the following week, the group leader explains their conclusions, the rationale, and any action that they believe needs to be taken. The new team member is satisfied with the outcome. Once any agreed changes have been made, the leader speaks with the new team member, who confirms that they have no ongoing or further concerns, the matter is closed, and the details filed and reported in the annual ministry report to the church / trustees.

- A parent raises a concern about the way their child has been treated. The message is taken by the church office administrator who tells them that they will contact the group leader, who will contact them within 24–48 hours. The group leader calls the parent who explains the concern. The group leader records the details, apologises for the distress caused and agrees to look into the matter and arranges to call them back within two weeks. The parent is happy with this. The group leader e-mails the parent to outline the concerns as recorded and asks them to confirm that the record is accurate and complete and also provides details of the church's complaints policy. Having looked into the matter, the group leader meets with the parent to explain the outcome of their inquiries and any actions or changes that have been made as a result. The parent is happy with the outcome. The group leader explains that if they change their mind, they can make contact again to discuss it further or that they can escalate the matter to a formal complaint and reminds them of the complaints procedure.

- During a group planning meeting, one of the members raises a concern. Most of the group disagree with them but the group leader agrees to minute the discussion and suggests that the matter is discussed again at the next meeting, allowing time for all of the leaders to give prayerful consideration to the matter. At the next meeting agreement can still not be reached and so it is agreed that the matter will be raised with the elders or trustees who will make a final decision. Both the group leader and the concerned team member attend the meeting with the trustees and the issues are fully and carefully considered before a final decision is made. Even though the concerns were not upheld, the leader thanked the whole team for their prayerful consideration of the matter and particularly the person who raised the concern, emphasising the importance of discussing such matters openly and considering them carefully.

In each of the cases above, the situation has been resolved through open discussion and a full investigation was not required. The key elements are:

- ensure that the concern is clearly understood and fully considered.
- ensure that the discussion and decisions are recorded.
- ensure that the complainant is satisfied with the process and that they understand that they can escalate to a formal complaint if they wish to.
- the concern raised is viewed positively as an opportunity to examine practice and make improvements where these are required.
- the complainant is fully involved and kept fully informed.

Complaint: Internal Investigation or Response Required

- The parent of a young person attending the children's group makes a complaint. The complaints procedure is provided to them (via a link on the website). The complainant expresses the desire to progress the complaint through the formal route.
- A concern raised with the elders or trustees by a ministry team leader who describes an unhealthy culture within the ministry area. They describe the public belittling and humiliation of women and younger team members by some of the established leaders. The trustees ask the leader of the children's work, which is unconnected to the youth group to investigate, supported by a trustee and a member of the congregation who has experience of conducting investigations into staff misconduct in their professional life.
- An individual is banned from accessing the church's food bank due to repeated abuse of volunteers while under the influence of drugs and/or alcohol. Numerous attempts

had been made to address the problems with them but they continued to escalate, with the police being called on several occasions before the ban was issued. The individual complains to the trustees. The chair of trustees asks one of the other trustees to review the records. They examine all of the records held by the church including the records of the incidents, the letters and e-mails sent to the individual, the records of discussions with them when sober, and the advice from the police. They conclude that the decision should stand and that there is sufficient evidence to make a formal investigation unnecessary. The trustee who conducted the investigation writes to the individual, explaining why their complaint has been rejected and informing them of the process and timeframes to lodge an appeal of the decision and explaining that they must explain their reasons for believing that the previous decision was flawed. An appeal is received which repeats the information previously supplied with a selection of angry and abusive insertions. The chair of trustees reviews the appeal and writes to the individual, indicating that there is no grounds for appeal. They reiterate the conditions that have previously been explained that will allow them to return to using the food bank and explain that the only remaining option is to raise the matter externally.

In each of the cases above, some action is required. Where a full investigation is required, the process would be similar to that followed for the investigation of a claim or allegation of malpractice. Since a complaint is likely to be about process, rather than an allegation against an individual, the process will reflect that difference, however the broad process will be the same as outlined above.

Complaint: External Investigation/ Learning Review Required

- An allegation of serious misconduct is made against the pastor of a small church. The leadership refers the matter to the police and the local authority, both of whom confirm that the nature of the allegations do not meet a threshold for statutory investigation and recommend following internal procedures. The only person in the church with both the prerequisite skills and the capacity to investigate the matter competently is conflicted as a result of being related to the pastor. The church decide to seek support from a larger church with whom they have long-standing fellowship, where there are several people with experience to conduct such an investigation due to their professional experience.

- Allegations are made of a culture of bullying of junior staff members and volunteer leaders, by the leadership of a church, over a prolonged period. The allegations involve all of the elders, who are also the trustees. A number of the complainants had experienced deteriorating mental health as a result, and some had resigned to avoid the pressure. The elders / trustees decide that since the allegations are against all of the elders, and the allegations are credible and not malicious, it would be unwise to ask a member to investigate, due to the perceived influence that they could exert, and so they decide to arrange an external review.

- Following a serious criminal or safeguarding breach, a church wishes to conduct a review of the culture to identify lessons that need to be learned. They believe that in order to look objectively at the culture, there is a need for respondents to maintain their anonymity and that a 'fresh pair of eyes' are required. They decide to involve an external organisation to lead the review.

In each of the cases above, the church is unable to investigate the matter independently or competently, so they seek external support. When considering an external review, the following aspects should be considered:

- The level of concern must be clearly established. If statutory thresholds for referral to the police or local authority have been met, the appropriate referrals should be made and no learning review should commence. The matter can only be investigated (either internally or externally) if the statutory thresholds have not been met. The investigation should reflect the fact that any offence is, by definition, sub-threshold.

- The purpose of the review must be clearly understood; is it an investigation that seeks to establish the veracity of the claims or is it to understand and learn lessons? A learning review should not normally be conducted until the facts of the matter have been established, otherwise the principles of just process will be undermined.

- Both the complainants' and the defendants' voices must be heard, and all of the information and evidence should be carefully considered within the context of the events, with careful attention to chronological development of the events.

- Clarity about the roles and responsibilities of both the reviewers and the trustees / leaders must be established.

As can be seen in this chapter, there are many complexities to handling concerns about pastoral malpractice. It is important that churches have appropriate and proportionate arrangements in place, and that careful consideration is given to developing a healthy culture. This guide aims to help you think through what is necessary, however, it cannot provide all necessary information.

Support and training are available for churches and their leaders in all aspects of safeguarding, including pastoral malpractice. A wide range of organisations, both local and national provide such training, however churches may find it helpful to access these from one of the specialist safeguarding organisations that are faith-based and have an understanding of churches, such as Christian Safeguarding Services[3] or Thirtyone:eight[4]. Both organisations provide a range of information and support to churches and also have information on their websites and YouTube channels.

CRIMINAL THRESHOLD MET

- The church receives a complaint that a church worker has been befriending elderly and frail members and stealing money and goods from their homes.
- The church receives a complaint that a youth worker has been using coercion and blackmail to obtain indecent images from children in the youth group.
- Indecent images of children and video of the sexual abuse of children are discovered on a member's computer.
- A pastoral care worker from the church is accused of befriending elderly people and coercing or forcing them to change their wills in favour of the church.

In each case above, the criminal threshold has been met. The church should immediately notify the police, taking care to ensure that any evidence is preserved. Any immediate action

---

3. www.thecss.co.uk
4. www.thirtyoneeight.org

to prevent further harm should be discussed with the police. They will also need to establish whether any immediate action is required to ensure the safety of everyone involved.

The church must then:

- cooperate fully with the police investigation.
- in the case of the youth worker, make a referral to the LADO (Local Authority Designated Officer).
- in the cases of the church worker and the pastoral care worker, consider whether a referral to Adult Social Care is required.
- inform their insurers of the fact that a police investigation is underway.
- consider how media interest will be handled and prepare a statement in line with advice from statutory services. This should then be placed on file in case it is required.
- consider whether a Serious Incident Report needs to be made to the Charity Commission.
- establish a clear communication plan that outlines what information can and should be shared with which groups in the church and how confidentiality will be maintained.
- consider what support can be made available to victims and how potential victims will be identified and notified of how to access the support.
- consider how the alleged perpetrator and their family will be supported through the process of the investigation and any legal proceedings that ensue.
- consider what support may be needed by members of the church or others indirectly affected.
- consider whether redeployment is possible, or desirable, or whether suspension pending the outcome of the investigation is necessary.

- consider whether any immediate changes to practice or staffing arrangements need to be made.
- consider how those directly involved in managing the situation, on behalf of the church, will be supported.
- all matters related to the situation, including conversations with statutory agencies, advice received, minutes of meetings, etc. should be maintained in accordance with the safeguarding policy.

*** Please note: the list above is not in priority order nor intended to imply a specific order of actions. This will vary from case to case. ***

Upon conclusion of the investigation and any subsequent legal action the church must:

- implement any follow-up action that is required or recommended by the statutory services.
- take any necessary disciplinary action (in relation to the person's employment, volunteering, or church membership) in accordance with their own internal processes.
- consider whether a referral to the Disclosure and Barring Service is required.
- inform the insurers of the outcome (if required).
- update the Charity Commission Serious Incident Report (if required).
- establish a proportionate review of lessons learned and implement any necessary changes (this will usually be an internal process).
- establish a process for communicating lessons learned and changes implemented.
- consider what ongoing support is required by those directly or indirectly impacted.

- consider how to best support the church to move forward from this point, seeking external specialist support and advice as required.

SAFEGUARDING BREACH IN RELATION TO A CHILD

Please note: these scenarios cover breaches by our own staff/volunteers. Safeguarding concerns that are disclosed or identified but which do not implicate the church are dealt with according to the church's own safeguarding policy.

- A children's worker fails to implement an agreed risk management measure (as laid out in the risk assessment) and an accident occurs as a result.
- A youth worker breaches the safeguarding policy by accepting a 'friend' request sent by a young person through social media.
- A youth worker is discovered in a small side / meeting room with a young person, discussing issues they are having with their (the child's) boyfriend / girlfriend. The office door is closed, and they are not visible to other leaders and none of the leaders had been informed of the conversation.
- A new children's work volunteer commences work in the group before their DBS has been received and cleared and references have been received. They are in a position where they have unsupervised access to children for a brief time and the policy clearly indicates that DBS checks and references must be received before the volunteer commences their role.
- The elders are dealing with a particularly sensitive pastoral issue involving a young couple with a new baby. As time passes, it becomes apparent that there is violence in the household, however, in their focus on the adults, they fail to recognise that there is risk to the child and do not notify the

safeguarding lead. As a consequence, the required referral to Children's Social Care is not made.

- A youth worker has been investigated by Social Services due to abuse and neglect of their own children. The children are now the subjects of a Child Protection Plan.

In each case above, the safeguarding procedures have been breached and consequently a child has been placed at risk of harm. Any resulting immediate risk must be addressed to prevent any further harm and the matter must then be reported to the appropriate person (as outlined in the safeguarding policy). The parents of any children involved will need to be notified of the breach, what immediate harm occurred to their child, what steps were taken in response, how the matter will be investigated and responded to, including when they will be contacted with an update on corrective action, who will contact them, and their rights and options relating to formal complaints or reporting to statutory authorities.

The church must then:

- consider whether a referral to the LADO (Local Authority Designated Officer) is required.
- consider whether their insurers need to be informed.
- consider whether media interest could result and if so, how it will be handled. If media interest is likely, a statement should be prepared (in line with any advice from statutory services). This should then be placed on file in case it is required.
- investigate the breach to identify how it occurred, what corrective action is required, how it will be implemented, including amendments to the safeguarding policy and procedures, disciplinary action that needs to be taken, training or development that is required etc. The

investigation should consider cultural as well as procedural aspects.

- consider whether a Serious Incident Report needs to be made to the Charity Commission.

- establish a clear communication plan that outlines what information can and should be shared with which groups in the church and how confidentiality will be maintained.

- consider what support should be made available to anyone harmed by the incident or their families.

- consider how those responsible for the activity, including anyone against whom potential disciplinary action may be taken or referral to statutory services may be required, will be supported through the process of the investigation and any resulting processes.

- consider whether any immediate changes to practice or staffing arrangements need to be made.

- consider how those directly involved in managing the situation on behalf of the church will be supported.

- All matters related to the situation, including conversations with statutory agencies, advice received, minutes of meetings etc should be maintained in accordance with the safeguarding policy.

Following completion of the investigation the church should:

- ensure that any follow-up actions required or recommended by statutory agencies are implemented.

- communicate the outcome of the investigation, including any changes made in response to those concerned.

- update any statutory or regulatory bodies and the insurers as required.

- review the process of handling the incident for lessons that need to be learned.

Safeguarding Breach in Relation to an Adult

Please note: these scenarios cover breaches by our own staff / volunteers. Safeguarding concerns that are disclosed or identified but which do not implicate the church are dealt with according to the church's own safeguarding policy.

- A church worker breaches the code of conduct by accepting an expensive birthday gift from an adult with care and support needs that they are supporting. The gift or the offer of the gift is not declared according to the processes laid out in the procedures.

- A church worker visits an elderly person in a care home and sees indications of neglect and physical abuse by the staff but does not report the concern to the safeguarding officer at the church and takes no other action to protect the residents affected.

- A church laptop is stolen which contains sensitive information about safeguarding concerns and contact details for adults who attend a group run for adults with learning disabilities. The computer is not password protected and the drive is not encrypted.

- A volunteer at the church's food bank offers to provide a client with additional provisions and preferential treatment in exchange for a nude photograph.

- The church runs a day centre for elderly and frail adults with care and support needs. The risk assessment clearly indicates a maximum number of attendees and ratios of volunteers to attendees which is based on the physical size of the room and considers emergency evacuation requirements and the levels of support required by those attending. The attendee limits and ratios are consistently breached due to the level of demand and the fact that pre-registration is not required.

In each case above, the safeguarding procedures of code of conduct have been breached and consequently an adult who requires proportionate protection has been placed at risk of harm. Any resulting immediate risk must be addressed to prevent any further harm and the matter must then be reported to the appropriate person (as outlined in the safeguarding policy). Those involved (and where capacity is compromised, their carers) may need to be notified of the breach and what steps were taken in response, how the matter will be investigated and responded to, including when they will be contacted with an update on corrective action, who will contact them and their rights and options relating to formal complaints or reporting to statutory authorities.

The church must then:
- consider whether a referral to Adult Social Care is required.
- consider whether their insurers need to be informed.
- consider whether media interest could result and if so, how it will be handled. If media interest is likely, a statement should be prepared (in line with any advice from statutory services). This should then be placed on file in case it is required.
- investigate the breach to identify how it occurred, what corrective action is required, how it will be implemented, including amendments to the safeguarding policy and procedures, disciplinary action that needs to be taken, training or development that is required etc. The investigation should consider cultural as well as procedural aspects.
- consider whether a Serious Incident Report needs to be made to the Charity Commission.
- establish a clear communication plan that outlines what information can and should be shared with which groups in the church and how confidentiality will be maintained.

- consider what support should be made available to anyone harmed by the incident or their families.
- consider how those responsible for the activity, including anyone against whom potential disciplinary action may be taken or referral to statutory services may be required, will be supported through the process of the investigation and any resulting processes.
- consider whether any immediate changes to practice or staffing arrangements need to be made.
- consider how those directly involved in managing the situation on behalf of the church will be supported.
- all matters related to the situation, including conversations with statutory agencies, advice received, minutes of meetings etc should be maintained in accordance with the safeguarding policy.

Following completion of the investigation the church should:
- ensure that any follow-up actions required or recommended by statutory agencies are implemented.
- communicate the outcome of the investigation, including any changes made in response to those concerned.
- update any statutory or regulatory bodies and the insurers as required.
- review the process of handling the incident for lessons that need to be learned.

REFINING TERMINOLOGY

The table on the next page is a useful tool for putting the term pastoral or spiritual abuse in the wider context of language we might use to describe other malpractice or criminal behaviour.

Analogies	Type of Offence	Commentary	GENERIC TERMINOLOGY
		PASTORAL ABUSE TAXONOMY	
		CRIMINAL LAW	
	Emotional & Psychological Abuse	Same existing category for all, religious & non-religious alike, whether in pastoral or non-pastoral contexts. These are illegal behaviours already covered by criminal law.	
		CIVIL LAW	
Medical Malpractice Misfeasance in Public Office incl. Abuse of Power	Pastoral Misfeasance	Applied to those in positions of pastoral leadership/responsibility, religious & non-religious alike. Medical Malpractice and Misfeasance in Public Office (including its sub-category, Abuse of Power) are civil offences. Issues may arise in independent church settings where churches do not formally ordain/license leaders or theologically apply ordained/licensed/lay distinctions.	Informally applicable across formal categories **pastoral abuse** spiritual abuse[1] abuse of religious power (lower case v. upper case for Civil offence of Abuse of Power)
		WORKPLACE DISCIPLINARY PROCEDURES, INSTITUTIONAL PANELS & TRIBUNALS	
Gross Misconduct Misconduct	Pastoral Misconduct	For leaders and team members/officers bearing formal pastoral authority – religious and non-religious alike. In general and secular contexts, to be addressed by HR disciplinary procedures. In religious contexts to be addressed by these and/or diocesan tribunals, denominational disciplinary panels, presbyteries, charity trustees etc.	
		INFORMAL OR LOWER-LEVEL CENSURE	
Bullying Manipulation Exploitation Undue pressure	Pastoral Bad Practice	For *anyone* who bullies, manipulates, or unduly pressurises others in pastoral contexts, distinct from any physical/sexual dimension. Applies to secular and sacred contexts and to religious believers and non-believers alike. Allows that pastoral leaders may be victims of clients, patients, congregational members etc. rather than perpetrators. **Preferred term to 'Spiritual Abuse' for this level of abuse.**	

Table by Rev Dr David Hollman – used with permission

1. As noted throughout this booklet, 'spiritual abuse' is at present the generic term most commonly used by analysts, victims and survivors to describe the range of negative behaviours detailed here. It appears vertically in the right-hand column in recognition of this. The same column shows 'Pastoral Abuse' more prominently, however, because of its wider applicability to duty-of-care breaches perpetrated by secular/'non-spiritual' pastoral workers, as well as by religious leaders and adherents. As such, 'Pastoral Abuse' is less discriminatory against religious or 'spiritual' people because it avoids the assignment of a potentially actionable offence to such people exclusively, with non-religious or 'non-spiritual' exempted, by definition, from that offence. The lower-case formulation 'emotional and psychological abuse' is sometimes also used generically to denote a whole range of criminal *and non-criminal* abuses, and this seems likely to continue until the more precise distinctions shown above gain fuller traction. While certainly preferable as a generic descriptor to 'spiritual abuse' because of its similarly non-discriminatory nature, this more generic usage of 'emotional and psychological abuse' is not shown formally in the taxonomy here because of potential confusion between these non-criminal applications of it and the specifically criminal offences of Emotional and Psychological Abuse (upper case), where Emotional Abuse is typically applied to children and Psychological Abuse to adults.

6

MEDIA AND ABUSE

Writing a chapter on media liaison would have been a relatively straightforward exercise a decade ago. A prescriptive set of 'dos' and 'don'ts' would have been followed by some specific pointed guidance.

While there are still some broad principles that stand; media relations have become very complicated in a very short period of time. This began to happen with the rise of the Internet, but has since exploded, with the rise of social media platforms and the ubiquity of tablets and smartphones for rapid access and response. It means that the lines between traditional media and new media have become blurred, and not everyone is playing by the same rules.

Let's begin with two definitions.

Traditional Media – By this we mean newspapers, magazines, television and radio. Usually, traditional media is staffed by qualified journalists working to a set of editorial standards and under the watchful gaze of regulators.

New Media – By this we mean online platforms such as blogs and Internet journals, as well as social media platforms such as Facebook and Twitter which are often used to publicise news from a variety of sources. This is where the lines are blurred, as all traditional media outlets now have an online presence.

It is relatively easy to navigate a relationship with traditional media. You have to be careful what you say, of course, but there are some ground rules that journalists work to. They work hard to get the story, but make sure they operate within the parameters of media law.

In new media, and especially with social media, you and your church may not be afforded the same courtesy. The Internet enables anyone to share their thoughts about anything with (potentially) a worldwide audience. Anyone can use the Internet to say anything about anyone or anything.

We need to commend what is good about this: the media landscape is now much more egalitarian, providing a space where multiple views can be expressed and debated. But the problem is that very few people operating in this sphere have media training which allows them to understand the law around slander, defamation and contempt of court. It would seem to us that breaches are so frequent, that no law-enforcement or regulatory agency can keep up.

In effect, this means the law is (rightly) enforced around serious criminal acts of racism, threats of violence, assault and the like; but that a judge in a criminal case in a court of law (for example) simply advises the jury to refrain from looking at online commentary of the case.

The point is this. It makes media liaison a completely different ball game compared to a decade ago.

SETTING THE CONTEXT

We need to start by reviewing the cultural moment we are living in, because this cultural moment shapes both traditional media and new media. In fact, you are much more likely to be called to respond via new media than traditional media when it comes to some of the issues outlined in this book.

The current focus of our contemporary culture is to deconstruct power dynamics. Be it race, class, gender or sexuality (to name a few), there is now a cultural assumption that those who have traditionally felt powerless should be empowered to change the narrative.

This is twinned with the pervading reality that was birthed in the sexual revolution of the 1960s which puts the individual at the heart of everything. Phrases like 'Be who you are' and 'The best version of me' and 'My truth' are now prevalent.

The result in the media space is that those with the least power (traditionally-speaking) get a platform and those who have personal stories to tell of self-fulfilment are publicised and celebrated. This is especially the case where their story helps to promote the views of those groups considered to be under-represented. The individual's experience helps to shape the narrative of an under-represented community.

Those who engage in the social media space are often vocal in and amongst an under-represented community. Here, in their Facebook group or Twitter-sphere their views are always affirmed and always recognised as right.

It is this culture of affirmation which helps us to understand something of the current media landscape. Increasingly, people are only consuming media that affirms their pre-existing worldview and assumptions. And on social media, you can always find someone who will. This idea of complete affirmation is intoxicating. And social media has enabled everyone to receive it.

Of course, this isn't all bad. As Christians, we should never want to see any human being considered less than any other – after all, the Bible is clear that everyone is made in the image of God. We need to be affirming our common humanity as the Scriptures teach us. We also want to give voice to the oppressed, and social media can provide a first moment of opening up about a situation where they might be afraid to speak in person.

But this all creates a very difficult media landscape for churches because the cultural narrative is clear. Churches and their leaders have always (traditionally-speaking) had power and therefore their views are less valid in contemporary culture than under-represented groups. Furthermore, churches do not fit the self-fulfilment narrative – in fact, the language of 'giving your life to Christ' is likely to be considered revolutionary – perhaps even dangerous and harmful because it is the opposite of 'be who you are'.

This cultural moment is also being used to question authority and leadership at any level. Disagreements and personality clashes are too easily labelled 'abusive'. The online community increasingly calls for churches to be 'safe spaces'. Increasingly we fear this means 'church that affirms me and does not challenge me'.

This media context is crucial. If you are going to engage in the media space in our current culture, you need a clear understanding of what you are stepping into.

It is naïve at best to assume Christians and churches can rise above this secular agenda when it comes to our own media engagement.

Shaping the News

It seems to us that in this cultural moment, the news is shaped not simply by what is going on, but rather the public's reaction to what we might call 'news events'.

Let's take an example from any morning news show on the radio. The news event is shared in a bulletin format. A comment is made by a protagonist to add weight to the story. But then the presenter adds: 'Let us know what you think.'

What follows is instant reaction to the news from the public which feeds the media output. It means the news is less shaped by experts who are asked to give a professional opinion, but by public feelings and emotional reactions to what people have heard. In turn, this shapes the ongoing narrative.

In effect, what was once the traditional letters' page of a newspaper is now a continuous commentary on the day's events via social media, instant messaging and comments boards.

The desire to deconstruct power dynamics (that we touched on above) means that the voices considered the most under-represented will be the ones promoted in the media space. This is increasingly happening in traditional media but is already the dominant narrative in new media.

In the days of 24-hour news and social media offering a constant commentary on the events of the day, there is no longer room for nuance. You are either right or wrong, on the right side of history or an ignorant bigot.

Are you ready to step into the media space?

Engaging the Media

This book has been designed to help churches to engage with accusations about abuse of power or so-called spiritual abuse. As we have outlined, these are likely to be matters that do not meet a statutory threshold and therefore (unless your leader has a wider public ministry) are unlikely to be covered by traditional secular media. More likely, you will be asked to comment by the Christian media (traditional and new) or on social media. This is because the allegations may come directly from an alleged victim or an advocate who has gone public with their story in the online space. Social media and simple blogging platforms mean that across the media landscape there is the opportunity for people to publicise a matter widely, without needing to convince a traditional media editor of the story's weight and validity. This means your engagement with the media over a matter related to an allegation of abuse of power will need to be carefully weighed up and consideration given to the principles like:

- How widely has the story been publicised?
- Is it harming the message of the Lord Jesus and His gospel?
- Is it likely to cause significant reputational damage to the church?
- Will it cause concern to members of your congregation?

We would generally caution anyone who feels the need to leap into a media storm, especially on social media, to think very carefully before doing so. You are very unlikely to win the argument and even if you do, you will find that your detractors are not won over. In fact, they may portray your defensiveness as a further abuse of power.

Further, we would only advise you to engage with the media when you can humbly accept that mistakes have been made and you want to apologise for them. In other words, there is no point trying to defend yourselves, even if you think the weight of evidence backs up your assertion. Your primary responsibility is not to the Christian or secular media, but to your church, and to the individuals – whether alleged victims or perpetrators.

There is no agreed definition of spiritual abuse, so you would be defending a concept that nobody has agreed on. This is tantamount to nailing jelly to the wall. Alleged victims of spiritual abuse will self-identify as such. By defending your position as a church or as a leader, you are questioning their felt experience. Furthermore, those who identify as spiritual abuse victims will be plugged into social media sources that validate their position. This simply means that if you enter the discussion to defend yourself, you are likely to face criticism from all those in the online space speaking up for victims, whatever the circumstances of the allegation.

Would you do this in any other pastoral situation – even if you disagreed with the way it was presented?

For example, the FIEC recently produced a resource for Ministry Wives which received some hugely negative publicity on social media. This came from egalitarian Christians who described the work as misogynistic and tone-deaf.

FIEC didn't engage. Why? Because those making the criticism are not FIEC members or in FIEC member churches. Rather, they are people who have already made up their mind about FIEC and consider their complementarian theology to be toxic. By engaging with the social media debate they felt they would not have changed people's opinions, but would simply have fuelled the fire. The 'storm' lasted around forty-five minutes on Twitter. FIEC churches did not expect comment, and they made a decision not to feed the fire. In our current culture there is wisdom in saying nothing, even if the comments are unfair.

There may be occasions when the online questions aimed at you seem reasonable, fair-minded and genuine. In these circumstances we would advise you to take the conversation 'offline' by which we mean to pick it up privately via email, phone or face-to-face. Even if a debate seems reasonable on social media, it can easily be hijacked so we would not recommend handling it in the public space of social media accounts.

To Engage in the Traditional Media

Sometimes it may be necessary to make a statement regarding a safeguarding or potentially criminal allegation, or something where there is already some degree of public knowledge and engagement. In those cases, where media or other public interest could occur, it is wise to prepare a statement in advance, rather than trying to develop a comment under pressure of time from a journalist or other individual. Where a statutory service is involved they will advise on the content of such a statement. If no statutory services are involved, advice can be sought from your specialist safeguarding adviser. This statement must not divulge or confirm any personal or sensitive information and will simply state what is happening. It will be brief and to the point.

Where there is public interest, a careful balance needs to be struck between:

- providing opportunity to gather additional information and evidence.
- maintaining the integrity of the process.
- maintaining appropriate confidentiality without compromising accountability and transparency.

Where there is public interest, and particularly when there is public pressure, there will be numerous pressures and temptations; all of which must be resisted. These include:

- denial, disbelief, or minimisation of the problem.
- jumping to conclusions.
- focusing on the reputation of the organisation instead of justice for all involved.
- shortcutting due process.
- making hasty or rash decisions.
- acting from a sense of being overwhelmed or panicked.

The best way to balance these, and to protect the reputation is to act with humility, upholding justice and acting with transparency and accountability.

It is worth also remembering the 'golden hour' principle. This common-sense principle borders on stating the obvious but is often lost in such situations. The decisions that we take at the very start of the process will impact the course and outcomes of the process, so we need to make sure that the decisions we make are sound and do not compromise the principles of justice and the integrity of the response. Remember the basic principle; if I am navigating and I plot a course that is one degree off, it won't make much difference now, and may be virtually indiscernible, but by the time I've travelled a thousand miles, I will be a long way away from where I planned to be.

There will be times when the media clamour is such that you need to make a response. This might especially be the case where a church has removed a leader from ministry or conducted an enquiry which has concluded that significant changes need to be made. In these cases, you can take advantage of the new media space by making a statement available on your website in response to the matters raised. We never advise conducting media interviews in matters of this nature, instead take your time to craft a good public statement. Your statement should cover all the matters you wish to address and not leave room for misunderstanding or give cause for follow-up questions. Vague statements which don't address the matters raised are to be avoided at all costs. You should make sure you adopt a humble tone and clearly state the things you got wrong, apologising for them, and outlining the things that will change, in light of decisions taken.

Here are a couple of examples to explain what this looks like. The following is a poor example of a public statement:

At Anytown Evangelical Church, we know that some people have been disappointed with the way we handled recent events. We are sorry if that's the case and will endeavour to do better.

This is littered with mistakes from a public relations perspective. Who was disappointed? With what? What are the 'recent events' you refer to? What will you do better? You should never say you are sorry 'if' as this infers that the person you are apologising to is some way at fault.

Rather, you statement should be much more pointed and specific. Here is an example of a strong statement:

> Pastor XY was asked to step down from his role as senior leader at Anytown Evangelical Church because he had exercised controlling behaviour towards members of the congregation. This included misusing passages of Scripture to strengthen his position as lead pastor and place impossible burdens on church members.
>
> As a church, we want to wholeheartedly apologise to the victims who have been affected by this style of leadership. We recognise that this is not the pattern laid down for us, of a servant-hearted shepherd, in the Bible. We are sorry for taking so long to accept this and know there are many victims who have been harmed.
>
> We have now put robust checks and balances in place with regards to our policies and procedures to try and ensure this could not happen again. In the meantime, if there are others who were victims of Pastor XY's leadership whom we have not spoken to, we would encourage you to come forward so that we can offer you a personal apology and any help you need to process your experience.

POLICIES AND PROCEDURES

Earlier in this guidebook we outlined some suggestions on policies and procedures that churches should have in place to help them address allegations of abuse of power.

To conclude this chapter on media engagement, I would suggest you consider a Media Policy – especially one which encompasses social media. Using some of the recommendations in this chapter, it will give you a framework to consider regarding when to engage in the media space and give you clarity on who should be responsible for that engagement.

A Media Policy does not need to be long or onerous but could helpfully consider things like:

- who manages the church social media accounts?
- when should a response be made?
- who should be a spokesperson to the traditional media?
- who will be responsible for public-facing stories or statements?

To do this thinking will serve your church well in wider media engagement in any event. To be forced to think about it quickly, if there is a need to make a public statement, is likely to lead to a mistake or misstep.

Let's end where we started. The media landscape is ever-changing, and we need to be wise to the reality that the way the media looks today is completely different to the way it looked a decade ago. This touches on our reflections about power dynamics. Traditionally, the big newspapers and media conglomerates had all the power. They don't anymore – but that reflects our changing culture and challenges it brings.

Sometimes the media landscape might feel unfair. When it does, we need to follow in the footsteps of the Lord Jesus and entrust ourselves to the one who judges justly (1 Pet. 2:23).

May the Lord give us wisdom in all our engagement.

CONCLUSION

In many ways this book is too long, in others too short.

The category of abuse of power is a biblical one, and the way to identify, investigate and deal with sin in this area is laid out in Scripture and is not complicated.

But on the other hand, individual cases are complex and every one of them seems to be unique. You may have reached the end of this book (and well done if you have) and you want to exclaim 'who is equal to the task?'

But let us give you four encouragements as you close the book and get on with life in your messy church.

PRAY FOR WISDOM
You might be daunted with the idea of judging the behaviour of a group and helping to reconcile and rehabilitate the wounded. You need the wisdom that comes from above. Ask the Lord for it.

BE SPIRITUAL
There is a spiritual dimension to every case you deal with. There is a spiritual battle going on with all the people you are engaged

with. This is not a simple gathering of facts. Truth does matter, but all of us are not truth telling machines but complex people whose affections need to be stirred.

REMEMBER THE GOSPEL

You will need to remember the gospel. When you fail. When you discover failure. The gospel at work in your heart and in all those who believe. The gospel that offers love to the guilty, the wounded and the unbelieving. Readily, encourage, offer and receive grace and forgiveness.

PUT CHRIST FIRST

The reputation you want to preserve should be Christ's. The name to be honoured should be Christ's. For all our failures He is the perfect leader and the perfect son and wherever we end up in these messy processes, if we are in Christ, we are safe.

We pray even through this humble resource, that the Lord might be building His church for the glory of His name.

CONTRIBUTORS

Colin Berg is a former Chief Executive of a local authority in Wales, and was previously Head of both Children and Adult Services in a local authority in England. When Colin retired he became a trustee with CCPAS (now 31:8). He ended his time there in 2016. Colin currently co-pastors Little Mill Baptist Church in Monmouthshire, South Wales, and is the Safeguarding Adviser to the Associating Evangelical Churches of Wales (AECW).

Jen Charteris is Executive Director of Crosslands, serving churches with in-context theological training and resources for ministry and mission. She made the move to Crosslands in 2018 after more than 25 years working in organisational, leadership consulting for government and the private sector. A trustee of UCCF and Stewardship, she also continues to speak on organisation, leadership, and governance for ministries around the world, including IFES and ELF. Originally from

South Africa, she is married to Hugo, a church pastor and planter in Newcastle.

Revd Ralph Cunnington lectured in law before training as a pastor at Union School of Theology, and Westminster Seminary London. He is pastor of City Church Manchester. Ralph is a published author, on the steering groups of Crosslands, 9:38 and UCCF. He is also a catalyst for the Northern Gospel Project – a church planting initiative.

Paul Harrison is a former manager of a SureStart programme in the most deprived area of Leicestershire. He had the lead for safeguarding across the locality and across the Leicestershire programme. He has also been in the Local Authority Designated Officer (LADO) role advising schools, investigating and responding to allegations against school staff and adults who work with children and young people in another local authority team. Paul founded Christian Safeguarding Services with his wife, Sue. He is also a preaching elder in an independent evangelical church in Loughborough.

Sue Harrison coordinates the training for Christian Safeguarding Services. She's a Team Manager for a local authority's Learning and Development team. Sue works in children's services and manages the newly qualified social workers training programme and the progression pathway for social workers. Sue supports CSS in advising churches on the various levels of safeguarding and competencies they need. She also manages the trainers' network for the CSS as well as delivering training to churches herself.

Revd Dr David Hilborn was until recently Principal of Moorlands College in Dorset. Prior to taking up this role, he was Principal of

St John's College Nottingham from 2012 to 2018, and Principal of the North Thames Ministerial Training Course and Assistant Dean of St Mellitus College from 2006 to 2012. David was Head of Theology at the Evangelical Alliance from 1997 to 2006 and an Associate Research Fellow of the London School of Theology between 2000 and 2012. He led three URC congregations before joining the Church of England in 2002, and served for ten years on the CofE's Faith and Order Commission. David has written and edited a number of books. He has written, published and presented papers on the topic of spiritual abuse.

Elinor Magowan studied History and Law then worked as a Solicitor, then a UCCF Staff Worker. She is married to David and has been a ministry wife in Whitby North Yorkshire and at Carey Baptist Church in Reading. For four years she was the Women's Pastoral Worker at UFM Worldwide but is now working as the FIEC's Director for Women's Ministry.

Revd Graham Nicholls is Director of Affinity, an organisation seeking to promote Christian unity and partnership of about 1,200 churches and Christian organisations throughout the British Isles. He is also one of the pastors at Christ Church Haywards Heath in West Sussex, UK. Prior to being in full-time pastoral ministry, Graham trained as an engineer and worked in the process control and computer industries with various computer technology companies in the UK and Europe in senior management roles.

Revd Philip Swann began ministry in West Yorkshire in 1990 after leaving his career in Cardiff as a Physiotherapist. He is now the Pastor at Llanelli Free Evangelical Church in West Wales. He also teaches Pastoral Theology, for the Evangelical Movement of

Wales, on their Theological Training Course. He also heads up the Soul Care Network for the Wales Leadership Forum.

Phil Topham started working for FIEC in the role of Head of Communication, but then became Executive Director at the start of 2019. Before taking up his position with FIEC he used to read the news for Heart FM in North Wales and has worked as a football commentator and reporter. He has also worked with the Anglican Church as Communication Officer for the Diocese of St Asaph.

Other books published by Christian Focus ...

NO MORE HURTING
LIFE BEYOND SEXUAL ABUSE
GWEN PURDIE

ISBN: 978-1-85792-679-8

No More Hurting
Life Beyond Sexual Abuse
Gwen Purdie

To many of us sexual abuse is a bewildering and deeply uncomfortable topic. News reports on the issue are greeted with a shake of the head as we think of the damage done, however in most cases, as the news continues, our minds gratefully move on to more comfortable areas. What do we do when we are faced with someone who has suffered abuse? - Or if you yourself have suffered abuse?

This book is a thoroughly Christian response to issues surrounding sexual abuse and shouts that there is LIFE after abuse. It is a frank look at a complex situation that affects more people than we would want to believe. It shows how to deal with many of the symptoms that those who have been abused are likely to suffer.

RELATIONSHIPS

HOW DO I MAKE THINGS RIGHT?

SHARON DICKENS
SERIES EDITED BY MEZ McCONNELL

ISBN: 978-1-5271-0471-6

Relationships
How Do I Make Things Right?
Sharon Dickens

We all have relationships – with parents, siblings, partners, friends. And all of our relationships are, in some way, broken. We mess things up, they mess things up, people get hurt. The Bible has a lot to say about how we should relate to other people, how to make things right when we've done something stupid and what we should do when someone has hurt us. But most importantly it tells us to make sure that our relationship with Jesus comes first, and that everything else flows from there.

PRACTICAL WISDOM
THE
PASTOR'S
LIFE
FROM THE PURITANS

MATTHEW D. HASTE
& SHANE W. PARKER

FOREWORD BY SINCLAIR B. FERGUSON

ISBN: 978-1-5271-0367-2

The Pastor's Life
Practical Wisdom from the Puritans
Matthew D. Haste and Shane W. Parker

The men whose stories appear in this book made up a network of pastors. Through personal contact, or by reading each other's books, they were bound together in a spiritual brotherhood and shared a burden to see God glorified, his Son magnified, and his Spirit honoured by wholesome and practical biblical preaching, wise pastoral counselling, church and family strengthening, and faithful Christian living. The modern church can learn from these men and their theology.